BEDFORD COUNTY, PENNSYLVANIA

1779 Tax List
and
1784 Census

HERITAGE BOOKS
2007

HERITAGE BOOKS
AN IMPRINT OF HERITAGE BOOKS, INC.

Books, CDs, and more—Worldwide

For our listing of thousands of titles see our website
at
www.HeritageBooks.com

Published 2007 by
HERITAGE BOOKS, INC.
Publishing Division
65 East Main Street
Westminster, Maryland 21157-5026

Copyright © 1989 F. Edward Wright

All rights reserved. No part of this book may be reproduced or transmitted in any form or by any means, electronic or mechanical, including photocopying, recording or by any information storage and retrieval system without written permission from the author, except for the inclusion of brief quotations in a review.

International Standard Book Number: 978-1-58549-151-3

CONTENTS

Introduction v

Bedford County Tax List of 1779
Bedford Township 1
Cumberland Valley Township 3
Turkeyfoot Township 5
Brothers Valley Township 8
Colerain Township 11
Hopewell Township 14
Ayr Township 17
Bethel Township 19
Dublin Township 24
Barree Township 28
Quemahoning Township 31
Frankstown Township 33

Bedford County Census Returns - 1784
Bedford Township 35
Colerain Township 39
Dublin Township 42
Milford Township 44
Barree Township 46
Bethel Township 48
Huntingdon Township 51
Frankstown Township 53
Sherley Township 55
Hopewell Township 59
Quemahoning Township 60
Ayr Township 63
Brothers Valley Township 65
Providence Township 69
Cumberland Valley Township 71

Index 75

INTRODUCTION

The following persons were taxed:
(1) Householders or landholders including land owners and tenants - no distinction was made between the two.
(2) Inmates, meaning residents in the household of another (not a renter) who worked for the landowner.
(3) Freemen, who were single men over the age of 21. Their names appear at the end of the listing of the township. All freemen were assessed the same amount.
(4) Non-residents, unseated landowners (unoccupied land).

These listings were taken exactly as written in the published Third Series of Pennsylvania Archives. The spelling of names has not been changed.

F. Edward Wright
Westminster, Maryland

BEDFORD COUNTY TRANSCRIPT - 1779

Bedford Township

	Acres	Horses	Cattle	Sheep
Thomas Smith, Esq'r	1,309	1	---	---
George Woods, Esq'r	1355	7	19	---
Thomas Anderson	---	1	1	2
John Andrew May	---	2	2	---
Solomon Adams	---	1	3	3
James Anderson	250	4	13	4
James Anderson	---	1	1	---
Robert Adams, Jun'r	100	3	3	4
Elijah Adams	50	---	---	---
James Beatty	---	1	2	5
John Bonnet	400	5	15	15
William Blair	---	3	3	2
John Bayard	300	---	---	---
Thomas Blackburn	100	2	2	---
John Bowser	150	3	3	2
George Burkett	---	1	4	---
Charles Brookens	150	---	---	---
Jonathan Cesna	200	---	---	---
William Cowen	50	2	3	3
John Crisman	150	---	---	---
William Clark	100	3	6	---
Thomas Croyl	---	2	3	10
Adam Croyl	100	---	---	---
Richard Delapt	---	2	4	7
Eliezer David	---	---	1	---
Henry Didier	---	3	2	---
James Dunlap	100	---	---	---
John Debert	200	3	2	3
Michael Debert	144	2	8	3
Samuel Davison	---	4	7	15
Samuel Drennon	300	2	3	4
James Dalton	80	3	4	3
David Irwin	---	2	3	2
David Espy, Esq'r	---	1	2	---
William Eckles	---	2	1	---
Adam Earnist	100	2	2	2
John Ewalt	265	2	10	1
John Ellinger	200	2	2	---
Joseph Eachart	---	3	4	5
Frederick Egy	---	1	2	---
George Funk	---	1	6	9
James Flatcher	150	3	3	---
John Ford	---	1	2	1
Jacob Feather	200	2	3	---
George Feather	100	2	2	---
John Graham	100	2	2	---
Robert Gibson	---	1	2	---
John Grigg	100	2	2	---
James Gordon	200	---	---	---
Jacob Harsh	---	---	1	1
Adley Hemphill	460	2	3	---
Patrick Hartford	---	1	---	1

Bedford Township	Acres	Horses	Cattle	Sheep
David Hoy	146	---	---	---
James Henry	250	6	7	---
Ditto for Wm. Henry	---	---	---	---
John Hite	---	---	2	3
Tho's Hay	200	1	2	---
George Imler	50	4	7	7
Honacle Iler	---	1	2	---
Jacob Iler	100	2	6	2
John Johnston	---	1	1	---
John Kasebear	300	3	3	10
Ditto	---	---	---	---
Thomas Kenton	150	2	2	---
Rachel Kenton	150	2	2	2
John Kenton	150	2	1	---
Benjamin Loan	---	3	2	---
John Lafferty	---	2	3	4
Levi Andrew Levi	600	---	---	---
Jacob Miller	---	---	---	---
George Millegan	300	2	4	5
Samuel McCashlin, Jr.	150	3	3	5
William McCall	---	1	3	---
Nicholas Maky	---	---	1	---
Samuel McCashlin, S'r.	---	4	5	---
Arthur McGaughy	---	2	2	---
James McMullen	---	---	2	5
Cornelius McAuley	---	4	3	12
John Montgomery	300	---	---	---
Edman Millen	495	---	---	---
Ditto	300	---	---	---
Ditto	200	---	---	---
John Millor	300	3	3	1
Anthony Nawgle	---	3	5	6
George Nixon	---	1	2	---
William Neemire	---	---	2	---
John Peters, Doctor	---	2	4	2
William Proctor	100	3	5	10
Samuel Perry	150	---	---	---
John Porter	100	---	---	---
Charles Ruby	---	1	5	7
D'o by Adam Sam'l	---	---	---	---
Jacob Rine	---	1	1	6
Timothy Ryen	344	1	2	---
David Reinhart	140	---	---	---
Gabriel Rhoads	140	3	4	8
Frederick Richard	100	2	4	6
William Rose	50	4	4	8
Allen Rose	100	5	2	---
George Romick	290	2	3	---
Jacob Saylor	---	1	4	1
Luke Simpson	---	1	2	---
Samuel Skinner	---	---	1	---
Hue Simpson	---	1	3	2
Lenard Swigart	---	1	1	2
Tho's Smith, Esq'r	---	---	---	---
Henry Swagar	150	1	2	---

Bedford Township	Acres	Horses	Cattle	Sheep
Daniel Smith	---	2	1	---
William Scovel	---	3	2	---
Adam Samuel	50	3	2	3
George Sills	100	3	3	3
Conred Samuel	150	5	4	3
Peter Swopeland	---	1	---	---
William Satorious	30	2	3	4
Andrew Steel	100	2	1	---
Peter Stiffler	100	2	2	2
George Swagart	---	---	2	---
Peter Sticklet	---	---	3	---
George Smith	---	1	1	---
Phelty Server	---	---	2	---
Michael Sills	112	4	5	4
Peter Smith	---	2	2	3
Samuel Todd	---	4	6	---
William Todd	200	4	1	---
William Todd, Sen'r	---	2	7	11
John Todd	---	2	2	---
Henry West	---	5	9	9
Ditto for Nawgle's estate	170	---	---	---
Michael Wallock	---	5	4	---
James Williams	200	3	1	13
Reinhart Wolf	200	3	5	4
George Weiscarver	---	---	---	---
Jacob Willhelm	---	1	2	2
Henry Walter	100	---	---	---

Cumberland Valley Township

	Acres	Horses	Cattle	Sheep
Anthony Ashers	---	2	2	---
Jacob Aswalt	200	5	10	14
John Billieu	40	2	2	5
Thomas Boyd	100	2	6	10
Bryce Blair	300	2	4	3
Peter Buzzard	150	3	3	6
William Bell	50	3	3	10
Andrew Boreland	250	4	5	7
William Browning	50	1	2	1
Patrick Burns	300	3	5	13
Jonathan Bishop	100	4	2	---
Tho's Coulter, Esq'r	200	9	5	17
Charles Cesna	297	8	3	5
Joseph Cesna	250	---	---	---
Jonathan Cuningham	100	2	2	---
Evan Cesna	200	3	5	9
Robert Campbel	150	2	3	3
Shadrach Casteel	50	3	3	7
John Cesna, Sen'r	100	---	---	---
Thomas Casteel	---	1	1	---
James Compton	50	---	---	---
Richard Croy	---	1	2	---

Cumberland Valley Township	Acres	Horses	Cattle	Sheep
Jacob Croy	---	2	3	6
William Devour	100	3	6	10
Thomas Dickens	100	4	1	3
Dominic Donnald	50	---	---	---
David Dason	30	2	2	4
Richard Delapt	300	---	---	---
Cornelius Devour	60	---	---	---
Arthur Elder	---	1	1	---
John Elder	100	3	2	10
Edward Evans	100	4	11	10
Nathan Evans	---	2	2	---
William Elliot	140	---	---	---
Tho's Frazer	200	3	5	---
Samuel Findley	340	---	---	---
Jacob Fox	150	3	5	11
John Farmer	50	---	3	3
Thomas Harden	30	---	---	---
George Hiepeter	50	---	---	---
Joseph Hines	100	5	8	---
John Hines	130	6	6	8
Andrew Husten	100	3	6	14
Alex'r Huston	150	2	5	7
Richard Hardisty	---	1	2	---
Joseph Kelly	225	4	7	12
Ditto	300	---	---	---
Mathew Kelly	200	2	3	5
Richard Lamister	40	4	6	4
Laurince Lamb	50	3	1	4
Ditto	20	---	---	---
Ritchard Low	30	1	1	---
John Laisher, Jun'r	50	1	1	2
John Laisher, Sen'r	60	1	1	---
Thomas Laisher	50	2	2	---
Ludwick Libergar	50	4	3	2
Nicoles Liberger	100	3	---	---
Timothy Lamb	---	1	1	---
Joseph Morrisan	150	---	---	---
Edward Moran	50	1	1	1
John Morris	50	5	5	4
Isaac Neemyar	50	2	6	10
Isaac Plummer	50	2	2	---
Samuel Paxton	100	1	2	---
Daniel Rhoads	80	1	4	2
Jacob Rhoads	100	---	---	---
Joseph Rhoads	50	1	4	6
Frederick Roise	50	3	4	8
Thomas Rhea, weaver	50	1	3	---
John Spurgeon, Jun'r	---	---	1	---
John Switzer	100	4	4	6
Nathaniel Screechfield	100	1	2	9
Frederick Seever	50	2	3	---
Joseph Slidey	250	5	3	5
John Spurgeon, Jr.	50	2	2	2
Nathan Stansbey	100	---	---	---
Mathias Sheets	25	1	1	1

Cumberland Valley Township	Acres	Horses	Cattle	Sheep
John Tumbleson	125	1	--	--
Benjamin Tumbleson	100	--	--	--
Chrisman Tuckman	300	3	5	5
Frederick Tuckman	--	2	4	7
Jacob Valentine	50	2	1	--
George Vendoms	180	4	3	--
Philip Wagel	50	--	--	--
William Workman	150	2	2	--
Andrew Welker	50	2	4	5
Paul Wilker	50	1	2	1
James Young	50	1	1	--
William Purdue	100	4	6	18
Ditto	100	--	--	--
John Tumleson	300	--	--	--
Tho's Silverson	200	--	--	--
Jonathan Cesna	--	3	2	--

Single Freemen

William Young	--	--	--	--
Daniel Hanes	--	--	--	--
Zadock Casteel	--	--	--	--
Samuel Boreland	--	--	--	--
Frederick Fox	--	--	--	--
Edward Huston	--	--	--	--
Robert Huston	--	--	--	--
John Nemier	--	--	--	--
John Tuckman	--	--	--	--

Non-Residents' Land

	Acres	Horses	Cattle	Sheep
Robert Lusk	300	--	--	--
Edward Ward	50	--	--	--
Samuel Findley	200	--	--	--
Robert Culbertson	100	--	--	--
Gen'l William Thompson	300	--	--	--
Richard Peters	1,500	--	--	--
Leonard Hartlen	200	--	--	--
Doctor Ross	250	--	--	--
George Funk	100	--	--	--
Samuel Perry	150	--	--	--
William Wilson	200	--	--	--
Cox and Comp'y	700	--	--	--

Turkeyfoot Township

	Acres	Horses	Cattle	Sheep
Henry Abrahams	200	4	6	--
Gabriel Abraham	100	--	--	--

Turkeyfoot Township	Acres	Horses	Cattle	Sheep
Peter Ankeny	400	3	3	---
Christopher Ankeny	400	3	3	---
Thomas Abraham	---	1	2	---
Widow Allen	150	2	1	---
James Alex'r	---	1	1	---
George Bourke	600	---	---	---
Henry Bruner	200	---	---	---
George Bruner	300	2	1	---
Ulric Bruner	300	1	3	---
William Black	50	1	1	---
Henry Brown	100	2	2	---
James Boyd	---	2	4	---
Jacob Bernhart	300	---	---	---
Peter Booher	150	2	2	---
Thomas Sipes	150	2	5	---
Christian Crim	---	---	1	---
George Countryman	200	---	---	---
Abraham Cable	300	---	---	---
Joseph Donahe	40	2	3	---
Jesse Drake	---	1	2	---
George Drake	100	2	4	---
Oliver Drake	300	3	2	---
William Dunwoody	---	1	2	---
John Everly	200	4	6	---
John Everly, Jun'r	200	---	---	---
Frederick Eackert	100	2	3	---
Peter Everly	50	1	1	---
Andrew Friend	100	2	4	---
Charles Friend	---	---	1	---
Ruth Faith	---	---	1	---
Ludwick Fridline	150	3	2	---
James Gilmore	150	2	---	---
William Greathouse	200	3	4	---
Thomas Green	100	3	6	---
Edward Hamet	50	1	2	---
John Hiet	---	2	---	---
Harman Husbands	900	3	9	---
Isaac Hulen	400	2	2	---
Elisabeth Hulen	100	1	1	---
Charles Herman	---	2	1	---
Jacob Hartsel	50	1	1	---
John Jones	100	2	2	---
David Jones	100	2	2	---
Ezekiel Jones	100	3	3	---
Robert Jones	150	---	---	---
Benjamin Innings	300	4	11	---
Henry Enlows	300	5	5	---
John Kirkpatrick	180	---	---	---
Adam Keffer	200	1	3	---
Philip Kimble	150	---	---	---
Michael Keever	50	2	3	---
Martin Keever	50	3	2	---
John Kimberlin	300	---	---	---
Jonathan Luffborrough	50	1	---	---
John Luffborrough	50	2	1	---

Turkeyfoot Township	Acres	Horses	Cattle	Sheep
Jacob Lout	200	3	5	---
Daniel Lout	---	2	3	---
George Leinhart	400	---	---	---
Enoch Leinhart	50	---	---	---
Matthias Meris	2,000	---	---	---
James Mitchel	50	4	3	---
Patrick McNight	70	1	2	---
John Mitchel	50	2	3	---
Daniel McEntire	50	1	1	---
Susanna McAnary	---	---	1	---
Jacob Miller	---	1	1	---
Daniel Morningstar	150	---	---	---
Jacob Morningstar	300	---	---	---
Phelix Morgan	100	2	2	---
Frances James Moore	150	2	5	---
Joseph Mountain	200	1	3	---
Henry Noble	---	1	1	---
William Nicholson	150	2	4	---
Hugh Nicholson	50	1	1	---
Benjamin Pursel	500	6	6	---
Nicholas Parone	200	2	4	---
Charles Putten	150	2	1	---
James Pursel	50	2	2	---
Casper Pile	100	1	2	---
Elihu Parr	---	1	1	---
John Pursel	50	2	4	---
Robert Plunket	50	---	6	---
John Penrod	250	3	4	---
Abraham Pridebaker	100	1	1	---
Samuel Wright	---	1	5	---
John Read	150	3	5	---
William Rush	150	3	3	---
John Rhoads	300	---	---	---
George Royce	300	2	2	---
Elisabeth Royce	300	1	1	---
Lewis Rose	---	2	4	---
Jacob Ripple	200	3	3	---
Henry Wright	50	3	2	---
William Roberts	---	---	3	---
John Royce	600	---	---	---
Cutliph Rose	---	3	3	---
Henry Rhoads	3,250	---	---	---
Aaron Royce	150	---	---	---
Tho's Strahon	100	2	3	---
Daniel Storm	100	3	4	---
George Shaver	300	2	1	---
John Shope	200	3	3	---
James Spencer	150	4	7	---
Jacob Shaver	150	2	2	---
Nathaniel Skinner	200	2	4	---
Reuben Skinner	150	3	4	---
Samuel Skinner	---	---	1	---
Frederick Unsel	---	2	2	---
John Vanderin	1,150	---	---	---
Abraham Unsel	---	1	---	---

Turkeyfoot Township	Acres	Horses	Cattle	Sheep
James Wilson	400	--	--	--
Frederick Wymer	150	3	5	--
Michael Walter	100	2	2	--
Thomas Whitlock	--	1	1	--
Ludwick Young	300	2	1	--
Richard White	50	--	--	--
James Walker	--	--	2	--
John White	--	3	3	--
John Weymer	200	2	3	--

Brothers Valley Township

	Acres	Horses	Cattle	Sheep
Peter Augustin	50	2	2	--
Frederick Ambrosia	200	2	4	--
Frederick Allfater	200	1	5	--
Peter Adam	80	--	--	--
George Brights	100	--	--	--
Michael Beeghley	600	3	3	--
Ludwick Barkley	70	2	2	--
Peter Booger	50	2	3	--
John Booger	300	2	4	--
Abraham Bridenburgh	50	1	--	--
James Barker	150	2	2	--
Christian Barkey	100	1	1	--
Stophel Bowman	100	1	2	--
John Benford	--	2	2	--
Jacob Bowman	50	1	2	--
Philip Baker	200	2	3	--
Jacob Berkey	200	2	2	--
John Berkey	--	2	3	--
White Blowith	150	1	2	--
Henry Bedinger	100	2	2	--
Michael Bair	100	2	2	--
John Borndrager	100	--	--	--
Philip Bedinger	--	2	2	--
William Cox	200	--	--	--
Abram Cahel	400	1	3	--
John Christner	100	1	2	--
Philip Cabel	--	2	1	--
Jacob Cabel	100	2	4	--
John Coleman	--	--	2	--
George Coleman	200	2	2	--
Christopher Cooper	--	2	2	--
Nicholas Coleman	100	2	2	--
Countryman's wife	600	3	5	--
Joseph County	100	--	--	--
Henry Davis	100	2	2	--
Casper Durst	200	--	2	--
William Dove	100	--	--	--
William Diver	600	2	6	--
Paul Drupe	200	--	--	--
George Drussel	--	--	2	--

Brothers Valley Township	Acres	Horses	Cattle	Sheep
Valentine Dralbaugh	50	2	3	---
Yost Deets	50	2	3	---
Clements Engle	150	2	1	---
John Etnier	250	3	3	---
Jacob Elberger	200	---	---	---
John Fike	300	4	2	---
Nicholas Foust	150	2	2	---
Adam Foust	300	---	---	---
Jacob Fisher	200	3	5	---
Henry Flake	100	2	2	---
John Furra	200	2	2	---
Joseph Furney	200	1	3	---
Peter Furney	50	1	2	---
Jacob Gabler	100	2	5	---
John Gittick	200	1	3	---
Solomon Gladfield	50	2	2	---
Jacob Glasner	300	4	5	---
John Groner	100	1	2	---
Henry Glasner	150	2	4	---
Arnd Grissing	80	1	3	---
Peter Graff	80	2	2	---
Jacob Good	200	---	---	---
Ditto	150	2	2	---
Witho Gamor	250	1	3	---
John Harshberger	100	---	---	---
John Hyder	50	1	1	1
George Hambough	50	2	3	---
Christian Hofstotler	150	2	2	---
John Hystotler	100	1	1	---
Adam Hoover	30	1	1	---
Jacob Hoystotler	50	1	1	---
Casper Hoover	250	2	3	---
Simon Hay	300	2	2	---
John Hover	50	2	2	---
John Hendricks	300	2	4	---
Christian Harr	100	2	3	---
John Hoot	400	---	---	---
Valentine Hay	---	2	2	---
Walter Hoyl	300	3	3	---
Joseph Jones	200	2	2	---
Jacob Jouler	50	2	2	---
Christian Knegey	300	3	3	---
Godfrey Knipper	100	1	2	---
Adam Koock	200	---	---	---
John Klink	50	1	2	---
Jacob Keffer	150	3	3	---
Michael Keffer	100	2	2	---
Peter Keever	200	2	4	---
Christian King	66	2	3	---
Valentine Lout	100	2	3	---
Peter Leep	100	2	3	---
Benedick Leamen	200	2	3	---
Peter Livingood	100	4	4	---
George Matthias	280	3	4	---
Joseph Mustler	100	2	3	---

Brothers Valley Township	Acres	Horses	Cattle	Sheep
Jacob Mote	100	2	2	--
Philip Matthias	150	2	2	--
John Miller	100	2	3	--
Michael Miller	100	3	2	--
Nicholas Miller	130	2	3	--
Frederick Mosstaller	30	3	3	--
Nicholas Miller	400	--	--	--
George Marker	50	--	--	--
Henry Marker	100	2	2	--
Jacob Millhouse	50	1	1	--
John Markley	400	5	7	--
Christian Miller	--	2	2	--
Philip Mason	100	1	1	--
Barnard Nawgle	--	1	1	--
Frederick Nawgle	50	--	--	--
David Noble	--	2	2	--
John (concealed) Ollinger	--	2	2	--
Adam Palm	150	2	3	--
Hugh Robison, Jun'r	150	2	2	--
Hugh Robison, Sen'r	200	3	2	--
John Stam	100	2	2	--
Frederick Saver	100	3	2	--
John Stump	400	--	--	--
John Saylor	200	3	1	--
Delman Sheets	100	3	3	--
Christian Spigar	300	3	4	--
Samuel Spiker	--	--	2	--
Casper Shrack	100	2	2	--
Christopher Stoner	100	--	--	--
John Switzer	80	--	--	--
Jacob Switzer	80	--	--	--
George Shaver	200	--	--	--
Jacob Shrock	100	--	--	--
John Shenifelt	50	--	--	--
George Shenifelt	300	4	5	--
Conrad Shallus	50	--	2	--
Boston Shallus	100	1	2	--
Philip Smith	50	1	2	--
Jacob Snider	50	2	3	--
Martin Sutter	50	1	1	--
Peter Switzer	100	4	5	--
Nicholas Shutes	100	1	1	--
Michael Tryer	100	2	4	--
Michael Tryer, Jun'r	50	2	3	--
William Tissue, Esq'r	400	5	4	--
John Tryer	250	2	2	--
Frederick Vantries	50	2	2	--
Peter Winger	400	4	6	--
Jacob Winger	300	3	5	--
Philip Waggerline	300	5	4	--
Jacob Walker	200	4	5	--
Yost Zuck	200	2	2	--
Jacob Zuck	200	2	2	--
John Zechman	--	1	1	--
Yeost Zimmerman	100	2	2	--

Brothers Valley Township	Acres	Horses	Cattle	Sheep
Christian Frick	200	---	---	---
James Gilmore	100	---	---	---
Matthias Mires	100	---	---	---
John Vanderin	300	---	---	---
Ditto	100	---	---	---
Ditto	200	---	---	---
Tho's Smith	300	---	---	---
John Vanderin	200	---	---	---
William Miller	130	1	---	---
Leonard Stam	100	2	1	---
David Griffith	100	2	1	---
John Griffith	100	1	---	---
Ebenezer Griffith	100	1	---	---
James Hendricks	300	3	3	---
Shaphat Dwire	---	---	---	---
Jacob Markley	200	1	---	---
Matthias Judy	300	---	---	---
Abraham Booger	---	---	---	---
John Bowman	100	1	1	---
Peter Layman	---	---	---	---
Andrew Baker	---	1	---	---
Jacob Fleck	---	---	---	---
George Graff	---	---	---	---
Jacob Hasson	---	---	---	---
Samuel Booker	---	---	---	---
George Miller	---	---	---	---
Christian Tryer	---	---	---	---
John Huntsman	---	---	---	---
Adam Ringer	50	1	1	---
Peter Bright	---	---	---	---
Frederick Coffman	---	---	---	---

Colerain Township

	Acres	Horses	Cattle	Sheep
Robert Moore	450	3	7	---
Peter Mires	100	1	1	---
Hugh Ferguson	100	3	7	---
Henry Livingston	---	1	1	---
Joseph Morrison	200	8	9	---
John Moore	100	4	5	---
Samuel Moore	200	3	3	---
Henderson Murphy	---	3	3	---
Tho's Hall	184	2	2	---
Tho's Burns	---	2	2	---
George Peck	250	1	3	---
Alexander Stamm	100	---	---	---
Tho's Reeves	50	2	1	---
John Buck	100	2	2	---
Abia Eakers	100	1	1	---
Andrew Jones	100	2	1	---
Philip Waggoner	100	1	1	---
James Murry	50	---	---	---

Colerain Township	Acres	Horses	Cattle	Sheep
Cornelius Simmons	60	1	4	--
Matthew Shwarts	100	2	3	--
Edward Daniel	200	3	3	--
Cornelius Seally	100	2	2	--
John Daniel	100	2	1	--
Nicholas Kegg	--	1	1	--
John England	100	2	2	--
William Beamer	200	2	3	--
Jacob Holtz	--	2	2	--
William Crissman	200	2	4	--
William Irwin	50	1	2	--
Francis South	50	1	2	--
Isaac Derimore	250	2	--	--
Tho's Pannel	50	2	3	--
Daniel Means	100	1	2	--
Joseph Sparks	100	5	6	--
Ditto	100	2	3	--
Matthias Holler	100	2	5	--
William McDaniel	200	3	6	--
Tho's McDaniel	300	2	2	--
Isaac Weymer	100	2	3	--
John Grath	50	1	1	--
Henry Tantlinger	100	1	2	--
John Shaver	280	2	3	--
Alex'r Murphy	50	2	1	--
Adam Weymer	100	2	3	--
Joseph Chapman	300	2	3	--
James Ridges	100	3	4	--
Benjamin Wigfield	100	1	3	--
James Barn	150	2	3	--
Tho's Alms	50	2	3	--
John Alms	50	2	3	--
Joseph Johnston	95	3	5	--
Tho's Johnston	50	4	5	--
Tho's Davis	50	2	2	--
Ezekiel Spurgeon	50	3	3	--
Samuel Spurgeon	50	2	4	--
James Stewart	100	3	1	--
Henry Amrine	100	4	4	--
Joseph Bennit	50	2	4	--
John Beaven	40	4	4	--
George Amrine	--	2	3	--
Samuel Moss	--	2	5	--
Tho's Hamilton	--	2	2	--
John Fleeharty	50	2	2	--
Robert Love	--	1	1	--
William Farmer	--	1	1	--
Michael Rufe	156	3	5	--
Ditto	344	--	--	--
Henry Whitstone	--	--	1	--
Daniel Collins	100	2	2	--
John McKeever	--	--	1	--
John Gibson	100	2	2	--
William Gibson	100	1	2	--
Margarit Gibbons	--	1	1	--

Colerain Township	Acres	Horses	Cattle	Sheep
William Forder	150	2	2	--
Joseph McFerren	150	3	4	--
William Russell	200	2	2	--
Reinhart Rippleogle	--	2	1	--
Adam Young	100	4	7	--
Henry Hines	100	3	2	--
Adam Miller	150	3	5	--
John Livingston	100	2	4	--
Abraham Covalt	300	3	4	--
Francis Reynolds	150	3	2	--
Amos Jones	50	--	--	--
Thomas Wood	246	6	1	--
Nicholas Rufe	250	2	3	--
Henry Williams	100	1	--	--
Patrick Heany	--	2	2	--
James Patterson	150	5	6	--
Casper Devonbaugh	265	4	3	--
John McClemens	250	3	--	--
Robert Culbertson	150	3	3	--
John Richey	500	2	5	--
David Buck	50	1	1	--
Joseph Cummins	150	2	1	--
John Boyd	100	1	1	--
William Boyd	300	2	1	--
Samuel Sampson	300	1	2	--
George Enslow	300	2	7	--
Tho's Arnet	150	1	--	--
Isaac Ceman	100	2	2	--
Christopher Enslow	--	1	2	--
Matthias Kelly	50	--	2	--
Henry Dervie	50	2	2	--
Frederick Hill	--	1	3	--
Isaac Amons	--	2	2	--
Robert Bradshaw, Jun'r	150	1	--	--
John Bridges	--	2	2	--
Robert Bradshaw, Sen'r	300	3	3	--
Tho's Bradshaw	--	1	4	--
Tho's Biddle	150	2	2	--
Earnest Baker	250	3	5	--
Laurence Coons	--	2	4	--
John Cesna	400	5	6	--
Jonathan Cesna	100	1	--	--
William Fredrigal	--	3	3	--
John Friend	260	6	9	--
Joseph Friend	180	4	6	--
Samuel Hall	--	1	2	--
Abraham Miley	300	2	5	--
Gideon Richey	246	2	5	--
Achor Worley	190	8	6	--
John Piper	400	5	4	--
David Ball	50	1	1	--
John Hagan	50	2	2	--
Edward Rose	100	4	6	--

Colerain Township — Single Freemen

	Acres	Horses	Cattle	Sheep
George Utzler	--	--	--	--
Martin Utzler	--	--	--	--
Henry Holler	--	--	--	--
Peter O'Neal	--	--	--	--
Henry Storm	--	--	--	--
William Bennet	--	--	--	--
Matthias Rufe	--	--	--	--
William Gibson	--	--	--	--
Hugh Means	--	--	--	--
John Russell	--	--	--	--
Francis Reynolds	--	--	--	--
Cornelius Ceman	--	--	--	--
Thomas Arnet	--	--	--	--
William Clemen	--	--	--	--
John Reeves	--	--	--	--
Thomas Williams	--	--	--	--
John McCormick	--	--	--	--
William Martin	--	--	--	--
Stophel Tripshoe, one still	--	--	--	--
Lawrence Coontz	--	--	--	--

Hopewell Township

	Acres	Horses	Cattle	Sheep
William Sampson	--	--	1	--
Ignatius Harden	50	2	2	--
George Shock	30	2	2	--
Jacob Miller	--	--	--	--
Joseph Phagan	--	--	--	--
Martin Stotler	--	2	3	--
Richard Kimber	--	1	1	--
Felix Miller	--	2	2	--
Tho's Miller	--	1	--	--
Hugh Skelley	--	1	--	--
Hugh Skelley, Jun'r	50	1	2	--
Michal Skelley	--	--	--	--
John Plummer	--	4	5	--
William Watson	--	1	--	--
Daniel Guthrie	50	2	3	--
Henry Sheats	200	2	2	--
John Enyart	100	--	--	--
Wm. Byser	200	3	3	--
Robert Whitnell	--	3	3	--
Mathias Mires	--	2	1	--
Solomon Sills	230	2	3	--
Stewart Anderson	--	2	1	--
Tho's Toberry	60	2	1	--
Samuel Thompson	150	3	1	--
Tho's Wilson	20	2	5	--
James Wilson	--	2	3	--
Jason Rutledge	--	1	2	--
Levi Moore	200	3	9	--

Hopewell Township	Acres	Horses	Cattle	Sheep
Michael Keith	100	---	---	---
Adam Keith	170	2	4	---
William Ebbit	---	1	1	---
James Cungham	300	---	---	---
Richard King	---	---	2	---
Charles Kam	20	---	---	---
Benjamin Sanders	300	4	3	---
Ditto	---	---	---	---
John Key	---	---	---	---
William White	340	---	---	---
Solomon Foshee	100	2	1	---
William Sherley	300	3	2	---
James Flora	40	1	2	---
Charles Clark	50	1	2	---
Joseph Johnston	---	1	---	---
Zebulun Moore	100	3	6	---
William Dean	100	3	5	---
William Arnet	170	---	1	---
John Shaver	100	2	2	---
Michael Dowlen	---	---	---	---
Hugh McCanna	200	---	---	---
Elizabeth Wilson	90	2	2	---
Thomas Edmiston	200	1	3	---
Susannah White	250	---	---	---
George Elder	180	2	2	---
John Covinhoven	100	3	5	---
John Weston	150	2	5	---
Philip Stark	100	2	2	---
James Hampson	47	3	4	---
Robert McGaw	300	---	---	---
Abraham Sills	300	---	---	---
Edward McGraw	300	---	---	---
Michael Kernahen	300	---	---	---
James McCardy	300	---	---	---
James Dean	300	---	---	---
John White	300	---	---	---
Francis White	300	---	---	---
Richard Dowlen	300	---	---	---
Tho's Dean	50	2	2	---
Richard Lilley	100	---	---	---
Ditto	---	---	---	---
John Dean	50	2	3	---
James Mullen	---	1	2	---
Hugh Hill	300	---	---	---
Peter Thompson	100	2	3	---
William Sherley, Jun'r	100	2	2	---
William Morgan	300	---	---	---
William Lean	300	---	---	---
Allen McClean	300	---	---	---
John Gatrill	300	---	---	---
James Bridges	300	---	---	---
Richard Sherley	100	1	---	---
Francis Gatrill	100	2	---	---
John Jenkins	100	---	---	---
Neil Clark	100	1	1	---

Hopewell Township	Acres	Horses	Cattle	Sheep
Robert Galbraith	1,200	--	--	--
Robert Trakes	--	2	3	--
Ezekiel Mobley	200	2	2	--
William Philips	200	2	2	--
William Bunn	150	--	--	--
David Ralph	100	--	--	--
Henry Hinesh	300	--	--	--
Anthony Kiger	100	--	--	--
John Morton	200	2	1	--
Hugh Guthrie	--	2	4	--
Abraham Plummer	125	1	--	--
William Smart	80	1	2	--
George Heater	90	2	3	--
Ditto	100	--	--	--
Frederick Shackler	100	--	--	--
Joshua Davis	--	3	4	--
Henry Hanowalt	300	--	--	--
John Oaks	100	2	2	--
William Anderson	50	2	4	--
Michael Whitstone	75	2	4	--
Jacob Shallus	50	1	2	--
Sebastian Shaub	200	1	4	--
Philip Stoner	100	2	2	--
Ruth Lewis	100	2	2	--
Benj'n Cherry	100	1	3	--
John Foster	100	4	2	--
Lewis Foster	100	4	2	--
Benj'n Kidd	100	--	--	--
Luesanda Piper	100	1	1	--
Wentle Hance	--	--	--	--
Tho's Buck	200	5	5	--
Ditto by imp't	100	--	--	--

Non-Residents

	Acres	Horses	Cattle	Sheep
John Allison	100	--	--	--
James Elliot	100	--	--	--
Samuel Hunter	230	--	--	--
Proprieter Manner	600	--	--	--
Baynton & Wharton & Comp'y	300	--	--	--
Joseph Donaldson	800	--	--	--
John Little	234	--	--	--
Reuben Hanes	900	--	--	--
Proprieter --	900	--	--	--
Col'n Boquet by 6 warrants	1,500	--	--	--
Daniel Clayton	200	--	--	--

Hopewell Township   Single Men

	Acres	Horses	Cattle	Sheep
Thomas Miller	---	---	---	---
John Euyart	---	---	---	---
Joseph Johnston	---	---	---	---
Abraham Plummer	---	---	---	---

Ayr Township

	Acres	Horses	Cattle	Sheep
John Anderson	---	2	3	---
Daniel Anderson	---	1	2	---
William Alexander	60	2	3	---
James Alexander	---	---	2	---
Robert Alexander	---	1	2	---
Jacob Adams	75	2	4	---
Robert Allen	---	1	2	---
Mathias Ambrosia	150	2	2	---
Margaret Arthur	---	1	4	---
William Alexander	---	3	3	---
Thomas Armstrong	---	1	1	---
Alex'r Alexander	---	1	1	---
Joseph Bell	---	3	6	---
James Brown	300	3	4	---
James Bell	---	1	2	---
John Buckley	---	---	1	---
James Bell	---	---	6	---
Tho's Barnet	---	1	1	---
Leonard Baugh	---	1	---	---
Roharty Bartholomew	---	---	---	---
Matthew Caldwell	---	---	2	---
James Cuningham	150	2	3	---
Edward Conner	96	1	1	---
William Conner	---	---	1	---
John Coyl	100	2	1	---
Bryan Coyl	---	1	1	---
Collin Campbell	---	---	1	---
Dougal Campbell	---	1	1	---
Henry Chapman	---	1	2	---
David Carlile	---	3	5	---
Lewis Davis	---	3	7	---
Henry Davis	50	1	2	---
Philip Davis	---	---	---	---
David Irwin	---	1	1	---
John Evan	---	---	2	---
William Graf	149	3	5	---
Ditto	55	---	---	---
James Gibson	---	3	3	---
George Galloway	---	2	3	---
William George	---	1	3	---
John Galloway	---	1	2	---
Edward Graham	100	2	3	---
William Gibson	---	1	2	---

Ayr Township	Acres	Horses	Cattle	Sheep
James Galloway	---	1	2	---
Robert Gibson	---	2	2	---
Samuel Kerr	200	2	3	---
John Kendel	200	1	4	---
Robert Kendel	---	---	---	---
Francis Slee	---	1	1	---
Anthony Lawson	---	---	---	---
Amos Stevins	---	1	2	---
Edward Head	150	6	14	---
Robert Hamil	---	2	4	---
Nathaniel Hammel	150	2	3	---
William Hunter	300	2	3	---
John Hamilton	---	---	---	---
Jacob Hoover	350	3	3	---
John Herod	---	3	5	---
Friderick Humbert	250	4	6	---
Henry Hoover	---	4	3	---
John Hoover	---	---	---	---
John Hunter	---	---	---	---
John Hammel	---	2	2	---
John John	---	---	---	---
Jacob John	150	3	8	---
Tho's Jackson	---	4	4	---
Tho's John	230	2	6	---
Tho's Lemon	---	2	2	---
Abraham Lowrey	---	1	1	---
Adam Linn	---	1	1	---
Francis Lee	---	1	1	---
Daniel McConnel	400	2	4	---
John McKinley	---	3	3	---
James Maxwell, Esq'r	100	---	---	---
Patrick Maxwell	100	---	---	---
John Martin	---	2	2	---
Daniel McCurdy	400	4	6	---
Daniel Myers	---	---	1	---
John McClelland	300	3	6	---
John McClelland, Jun'r	---	2	3	---
James McCormick	---	1	3	---
Widow McFall	300	3	3	---
John McClelan	300	---	---	---
Alex'r McConnel	---	3	3	---
Widow Nesbit	150	2	4	---
Widow Owens	50	1	1	---
Wentel Ott	---	2	5	---
Tho's Paxten, Esq'r	---	2	1	---
William Patterson	---	3	1	---
Evan Philips	100	2	6	---
John Paxton	---	2	2	---
John Query	150	---	---	---
Daniel Royer	205	3	8	---
John Rankin	290	4	4	---
Joseph Rind	---	4	---	---
Robert Scott	357	1	1	---
James Stewart	---	---	---	---
Thomas Stevins	100	2	6	---

Ayr Township	Acres	Horses	Cattle	Sheep
Evan Shelby	100	2	6	---
John Smith	130	1	4	---
William Swagart	---	2	2	---
William Salmon	150	6	7	---
Richard Steven	---	1	1	---
Ja's Liddle Simpson	250	---	---	---
Benjamin Stevens	---	2	2	---
Adam Shull	---	1	1	---
Stillwell Truax	100	2	4	---
Charles Taggart	92	2	1	---
Robert William	---	2	2	---
Hill Wilson	---	2	3	---
Charles Wilson	---	1	---	---
William Wilson	---	3	3	---
Stephen Winter	---	---	4	---
Enoch Williams	150	2	3	---
Conrad Wolfkill	---	2	3	---
John Willson	200	1	---	---

Bethel Township

	Acres	Horses	Cattle	Sheep
John Amil	50	1	1	---
William Andris	150	3	4	6
Benjamin Abit	250	4	12	19
Adam Ash	150	3	5	---
William Artt	100	1	2	---
John Burd	50	2	6	---
Jacob Brown	100	3	6	5
Thomas Brown	---	---	1	---
David Brown	300	5	14	11
Jacob Barrman	103	1	2	4
George Bishop	98	3	5	---
John Breathed	315	14	20	34
Christofer Bush	100	4	6	10
Henry Bruser	117	3	6	9
Thomas Crossen	130	---	---	---
Abraham Clevinger	80	2	7	8
Widow Carrs	---	---	2	---
Robert Campbell	---	1	4	---
Edward Combs	50	3	2	12
William Curry	---	1	4	---
Joseph Cobel	---	3	4	---
John Dart	50	2	2	---
Henry Dice	100	---	---	---
Gaven Eddy	100	3	---	---
George Enslow	300	---	---	---
John Fitspatrick	100	---	---	---
Robert Findley	---	3	3	3
Thomas French	400	2	8	8
John Fisher	153	4	12	12
John Fisher	100	---	---	---
Daniel Fikle	100	2	2	---

Bethel Township	Acres	Horses	Cattle	Sheep
Philip Gillelan	450	4	9	7
Moses Gordon	20	3	1	--
Ditto	100	--	--	--
John Guthrie	150	2	5	3
Samuel Graves	100	4	4	10
Widow Graham	200	2	5	--
Moses Graham	--	1	1	--
William & John Grahams	100	2	2	--
Albright George	300	1	8	5
Solomon Hull	--	1	1	--
Henry Haversack	150	--	--	--
William Hart	200	3	15	8
William Hart	150	--	--	--
William Hart	50	--	--	--
William Hart	150	--	--	--
George Hill	50	3	6	4
Jacob Hendershot	100	3	4	6
John George Hoss	100	4	8	11
Jacob Hough	300	3	9	4
George Hoop	60	3	3	--
William Hunt	149	4	5	5
Nelson Joyl	--	2	2	2
Evan Jenkins	184	4	4	--
Christian Kowell	250	2	3	11
Peter Kimble	--	--	1	--
Robert Kerr	200	3	4	--
Nicholas Leech	200	--	4	--
estate of John Lancaster, dec'd	300	1	2	--
Widow Lamb	50	2	2	4
Widow Lowder	300	--	--	--
Steven Leech	--	1	--	--
Levi Linn	--	3	5	7
Adis Linn	50	3	7	9
Isaac Linn	90	4	7	11
Widow Linn	100	3	18	16
Martin Longstreth	170	2	3	8
Bartholomew Longstreth	75	2	4	--
John Longstreth	--	--	1	--
Philip Longstreth	600	2	7	4
Christian Lance	50	1	2	--
George Lambert	300	--	--	--
Asher Leaton	100	2	4	4
Samuel Leaton	100	2	3	3
William Leaton	--	2	2	--
Obadia Leaton	50	3	3	6
John Mason	100	2	2	--
Widow Morehouse	150	1	1	--
Barnet Money	125	3	12	4
Edward Morton	60	4	9	6
William Morton	323	2	2	--
Thomas Morton	--	2	--	--
John Morton	50	4	7	8
Richard Morton	200	2	4	--
John Melott	--	1	2	--
Theodorus Melot	150	2	3	2

Bethel Township	Acres	Horses	Cattle	Sheep
John Melott, Esq'r	300	3	6	6
Obadiah Melott	100	---	---	---
James McKee	---	2	1	---
Jacob Money	150	2	6	9
Andrew Man	154	5	8	6
Andrew Man	100	---	---	---
Andrew Man	80	---	---	---
Andrew Man	150	---	---	---
Andrew Man	132	---	---	---
John McKinney	---	3	4	4
Joseph McKinney	300	3	4	3
George Moran	150	---	---	---
John McUne	50	1	1	---
George McClean	50	1	1	---
James McCormick	50	1	1	---
James McCormick, Jun'r	---	1	---	---
John Montgomery	100	---	---	---
Duncan McSparren	---	3	4	---
Robert McKinney	---	2	3	---
Michael Nehemiah	50	1	1	---
Henry Ongar	200	4	9	6
Richard Pittman	100	2	8	6
Joseph Pitman	---	3	5	16
Jonathan Penn	---	2	6	3
Joseph Powell	100	4	8	15
Richard Pitman	50	1	2	8
Richard Pitman	200	---	---	---
William Pitman	---	2	7	---
George Peck	150	4	5	10
Patrick Quin	---	1	1	---
Moses Reed, Esq'r	230	---	---	---
Moses Reed	103	3	9	13
David Rush	---	3	4	3
John Rush	173	4	16	20
John Reynolds	112	5	6	4
Francis Reynold	---	4	6	6
Peter Rush	100	2	3	2
Widow Rush	---	1	2	3
Jacob Rush	50	---	---	---
Henry Rush	150	3	8	8
Henry Rush, Sen'r	100	---	---	---
Henry Rush, Jun'r	100	2	4	4
Jacob Rush	150	3	3	2
Jacob Rush	50	2	2	3
Nathaniel Robony	81	2	3	---
Abner Reeves	---	4	5	---
Widow Slaughter	100	---	---	---
Michael Stall	400	2	3	5
Frederick Stitts	100	4	5	8
Henry Sousley	100	---	8	1
Laurince Sliker	113	3	10	3
Adam Smith	---	3	10	3
Peter Smith	136	4	11	4
Peter Smith	50	---	---	---
Alex'r Stam	---	---	---	1

Bethel Township	Acres	Horses	Cattle	Sheep
John Smith	178	2	5	--
John Smith	100	--	--	--
Henry Smith	300	2	2	4
Adam Snider	--	3	1	--
Jeremiah Stillwell	--	2	6	9
Elias Stillwell	300	4	27	17
John Stillwell	50	5	15	17
John Simmerman	80	2	3	5
Henry Snider	100	--	--	--
William Swells	--	2	3	2
John Shefer	50	--	10	6
Samuel Samson	--	--	6	--
John Stanley	300	3	5	2
Richard Stevens	--	2	4	4
Abednego Stevens	100	3	6	7
William Stevens	50	2	1	2
Charles Selly	--	3	6	--
Christofer Tittyheffer	--	1	4	10
John Smith	150	--	--	--
Henry Sipes	100	2	3	8
Harmer Shuller	100	2	2	2
Jacob Sock	83	2	7	--
Mathias Shaver	100	--	--	--
Jacob Shingletaker	100	3	2	--
Charles Sipes	50	1	2	9
Christofer Stover	--	1	1	--
Thomas Stafford	90	2	8	3
Emanuel Smith	50	3	3	--
Ezekiel Smith	--	1	1	--
Benjamin Truax	150	3	12	10
John Truax	100	2	3	5
Samuel Truax	200	3	6	8
Ditto	100	--	--	--
Jacob Truax	150	1	10	4
Philip Truax	50	5	6	12
Joseph Thrall	100	1	2	4
Ditto	100	--	--	--
John Whipkey	300	3	7	6
John Walker	250	--	--	--
Ditto	300	3	7	6
Hugh White	209	--	--	--
Joel Wright	100	--	--	--
Jacob Wenk	200	3	7	5
William Williams	120	1	4	1
James Warford	200	3	8	5
Henry Warford	--	4	5	7
Widow Warford	350	2	5	10
John Walker	154	--	--	--
Thomas William	60	2	4	11
Ditto	50	--	--	--
Robert Wilkey	50	2	2	2
John Walker	300	4	7	6
Henry Yeaky	--	2	4	5
Peter Yager	--	2	2	2
Bethuel Covalt	150	3	5	3

Bethel Township	Acres	Horses	Cattle	Sheep
William Carney	250	4	10	11
John Coombs	106	4	8	12
Dougall Campbell	---	2	2	8
Powell George	50	---	---	---
Elisabeth Stanley	---	3	---	---
Francis Allison	300	---	---	---
James Bringhurst	100	---	---	---
Ditto	100	---	---	---
Ditto	300	---	---	---
Robert Cumming	100	---	---	---
Edward Graham	100	---	---	---
George Frazer Hawkins	600	---	---	---
Conred Hockersmith	100	---	---	---
----- Jones	400	---	---	---
Benjamin Kidd	500	---	---	---
Philip Lipps	200	---	---	---
Jacob McClean	300	---	---	---
James McClean	300	---	---	---
Matthew Witeham	60	---	---	---
Daniel Ogland	100	---	---	---
Joseph Plater	100	---	---	---
William Head	100	---	---	---
Peter Head	100	---	---	---
George Shingledecker	200	---	---	---
William Welch	200	---	---	---
William Gates	150	---	---	---

Single Men

Tho's Martin	---	---	---	---
Jacob Rush	---	---	---	---
John Rush	---	---	---	---
Henry Sourley	---	---	---	---
Philip Truax	---	---	---	---
Alexander Stam	---	---	---	---
Moses Graham	---	---	---	---
Powel George	---	---	---	---
Samuel Thistle	---	---	---	---
Daniel Trench	---	---	---	---
Christopher Howdershelt	---	---	---	---
Peter Rush	---	---	---	---
Abraham Cowl	---	---	---	---
Robert Gray	---	---	---	---
Benjamin Morrison	---	---	---	---
John Curry	---	---	---	---
James Curry	---	---	---	---
Tho's McGee	---	---	---	---
Wm. Eddy	---	---	---	---
John Walker	---	---	---	---
Michael Shingletaker	---	---	---	---
George Onger	---	---	---	---

Dublin Township

	Acres	Horses	Cattle	Sheep
George Ashman	700	8	8	--
Alexander Anderson	--	1	2	--
Daniel Anderson	--	1	1	--
John Appleby	50	2	2	--
Eleanor Armstrong	60	1	1	--
Thomas Bird	100	2	1	--
Thomas Blair	100	3	3	2
Benjamin Briggs	150	--	2	--
Samuel Bell	100	1	2	--
Benjamin Briggs, Jun'r	--	1	1	--
Henry Burg	200	--	--	--
Samuel Briggs	--	2	1	--
Alexander Blair	--	2	1	--
James Barnett	160	2	4	--
John Bell	100	1	2	--
Andrew Barninger	100	1	2	--
Francis Brothers	40	--	--	--
William Brown	--	1	3	--
Benjamin Brown	--	1	1	--
William Bryan	--	2	1	--
James Bird	--	1	2	--
John Burd	150	2	7	--
Benjamin Burd	100	1	--	--
Charles Boyl	100	2	4	--
Henry Boyls	--	1	2	--
James Carmichael	150	3	4	--
James Coyl	150	3	3	--
Patrick Cassedy	100	1	2	--
Sam'l McMath	50	2	2	--
William Cornelius	--	1	1	--
James Cond	--	2	4	--
John Cornelius	50	3	4	--
Nicholas Coonts	50	2	2	--
Joseph Cornelius	50	2	1	--
Thomas Cole	--	1	1	--
Broad Coal	--	1	1	--
Patrick Cannon	--	2	2	--
James Clugage	100	2	3	--
Henry Canote	90	1	--	--
Gavin Clugage	300	3	5	--
George Clugage	300	2	2	--
James Canon	50	1	2	--
Hercules Camp	50	1	--	--
Samuel Charleton	60	1	2	--
Robison Chilcot	--	1	2	--
Batzer Copenhaver	40	2	3	--
Hugh Davison	200	4	5	--
Isaiah Davis	50	1	1	--
John Donache	50	2	2	--
Bartholomew Davis	--	2	1	--
William Edwards	--	2	1	--
Benjamin Elliot	100	2	4	--
John Elliot	150	--	--	--
James Fleming	100	2	3	--

Dublin Township	Acres	Horses	Cattle	Sheep
Patrick Fitsimmons	40	1	1	---
James Foley	200	4	5	---
Joseph Franklin	---	1	1	---
Nicholas Firestone	100	---	---	---
John Gallaher	100	1	1	---
Hugh Glenn	50	2	1	---
George Goosehorn	50	2	2	---
Jacob Goosehorn	---	1	1	---
Robert Gardner	---	1	2	---
Joseph Green	30	1	---	---
James Galbraith	900	4	4	---
Thomas Hunter	---	1	1	---
George Hudson	100	2	1	---
Henry Holt	50	2	2	---
William Hade	40	---	---	---
Thomas Hodge	30	1	2	---
William Holliday	---	2	3	---
William Justice	30	3	3	---
James Johnston	200	1	3	---
Robert Johnston	100	1	1	---
Robert Johns	200	---	---	---
Moses Kirkpatrick	---	2	1	---
William Kelly	20	1	1	---
James Lynd	---	1	1	---
John Latta	100	1	2	---
Dutton Lane	---	1	2	---
Jonathan Loveall	---	1	2	---
Corban Lane	---	2	2	---
John Long	---	2	2	---
William Long	---	1	1	---
Samuel Lane	100	3	3	---
Wilkison Lane	---	2	2	---
Benjamin Long	80	1	2	---
William Morris	300	2	3	---
David McMoultrie	125	---	---	---
Charles McGinnes	---	1	2	---
James Merdac	---	1	2	---
William Mason	---	1	1	---
James McKee	100	2	2	---
Andrew Michael	---	2	2	---
John Moore	50	2	2	---
James Morton	100	2	---	---
Alex'r McElroy	---	2	2	---
James McArdel	---	---	---	---
Jean McGill	100	1	2	---
James McPhetro	---	1	1	---
James Miller	100	2	2	---
Tho's Murphy	50	1	2	---
Nathan McDowell	150	---	---	---
William McDowell	150	---	---	---
John McCrea	---	1	1	---
John Morgan	200	2	5	---
John Mason	100	1	2	---
Manassah McClees	---	2	2	---
James McBride	40	1	1	---

Dublin Township	Acres	Horses	Cattle	Sheep
Royer McClelan	60	--	--	--
Matthew Patten	--	2	2	--
Hethcott Picket	--	2	2	--
John Pollock	40	--	1	--
Acquilla Keer	--	--	--	--
Robert Ramsey	150	4	5	--
John Ramsey	300	4	5	--
William Ramsey	40	1	2	--
Alex'r Rutter	--	2	3	--
Jacob Sharah	500	3	7	--
John Stitt	--	2	3	--
Casper Smith	--	1	1	--
Benjamin Standiford	--	1	2	--
Giles Stevens	--	2	3	--
John Sharah	100	1	5	--
Hugh Orlton	200	4	7	--
John Swagart	25	--	--	--
Zachariah Stevens	--	--	--	--
Thomas Stevens	--	--	2	--
Robert Strawbridge	50	--	--	--
James Shields	150	1	2	--
David Stiles	--	1	1	--
John Thompson	--	1	2	--
John Tice	--	2	2	--
Samuel Taylor	100	1	2	--
William Pollard	500	5	5	--
David Walker	100	2	2	--
John Walker	50	2	3	--
James Wilson	200	2	2	--
Paul Warner	200	2	3	--
James Wakeup	50	--	1	--
Henry Warner	170	3	3	--
Matthey Utley	--	1	2	--
George Wilson	60	2	2	--
William Winton	--	1	2	--
John Wilson	50	1	1	--
William Ward	--	1	2	--
James Wilson	60	--	--	--
William Young	40	2	2	--
Nicholas Welch	50	1	1	--
Francis Whiteinger	--	--	--	--
John Wane	100	--	1	--
Stevens Vincent	--	1	1	--

Freemen

	Acres	Horses	Cattle	Sheep
James Watson	100	--	--	--
William Weston	50	1	1	--
Thomas Weston	--	1	1	--
Domnic Dimon	--	1	--	--
Tho's Morgan	--	1	--	--
George Stanes	50	2	2	--

Dublin Township

Freemen

	Acres	Horses	Cattle	Sheep
William Carter	150	1	1	--
John Bell	--	--	--	--
Jonas Utley	--	--	--	--
Samuel Baker	--	--	--	--
John Harris	--	--	--	--
James Cannon	--	--	--	--
John Davis	--	--	--	--
Gaven Clugage	--	--	--	--
George Clugage	--	--	--	--
Benjamin Long	--	--	--	--
William Stanes	--	--	--	--
Tho's Carter	--	--	--	--
Acquilla Kerr	--	--	--	--
Samuel Morton	--	--	--	--
John Armstrong	100	1	--	--
Robert Nixon	--	--	--	--
Nicholas Goosehorn	--	--	--	--
Patrick Sullivan	--	--	--	--
John Kelley	--	--	--	--
James Love	--	--	--	--
William Hutchison	--	--	--	--
Tho's Clark	--	--	--	--
Robert Galbraith	--	--	--	--
Robert Kelsey	--	--	--	--

Non-Residents

	Acres			
Jeremiah Warder	230	--	--	--
Dr. Wm. Smith	200	--	--	--
Wm. Henry	400	--	--	--
Samuel Findley	200	--	--	--
----- Hunter	200	--	--	--
George Armstrong	400	--	--	--
Steven Duncan	200	--	--	--
Baynton & Wharton	500	--	--	--
Perry & McGaw	100	--	--	--
----- Lukens	150	--	--	--
Rev'd John Steel	300	--	--	--
Josiah Devonport	300	--	--	--
Wm. Buchannen	300	--	--	--
Jacob Wilson	300	--	--	--
John Elliot	150	--	--	--
Robert McGaw	300	--	--	--
Tho's Matthews	400	--	--	--
Gen'l John Armstrong	400	--	--	--
Tho's Blair	150	--	--	--

Barree Township

	Acres	Horses	Cattle	Sheep
John Armstrong	300	---	---	---
Hope Arthur	50	---	---	---
Samuel Anderson	300	2	8	---
Ditto	200	---	---	---
Ditto	200	---	---	---
Ditto	100	---	---	---
Ditto	60	---	---	---
Frederic Albugh	50	---	---	---
Charles Brotherton	---	---	1	---
Col. Bouquet	600	---	---	---
Benjamin Blyth	100	---	---	---
John Bready	100	---	---	---
William Bunns	100	---	---	---
Bensent and Jiles	600	---	---	---
John Bawser	---	4	5	---
Michael Crider	300	2	5	---
Daniel Carpenter	---	---	---	---
Francis Clugage	90	2	1	---
Nicholas Crafface	190	2	2	---
Peter Craflace	190	2	2	---
Daniel Clark	300	---	---	---
Charles Caldwell	200	4	3	---
Robert Caldwell	300	3	3	---
Jacob Canor	---	---	---	---
William Carr	150	---	---	---
John Cannon	100	3	2	---
Robert Criswell	150	---	---	---
Rachel Cox	300	---	---	---
John Cox	300	---	---	---
James Criswell	100	---	2	---
Moses Donnelson	100	---	---	---
James Dunlap	450	---	---	---
Samuel Daniel	60	---	---	---
Benjamin Drake	100	2	2	---
John Dickey	300	---	---	---
James Dickey	300	---	---	---
Widow Dick	200	---	---	---
Peter Dewit	---	1	1	---
James Dean	---	2	2	---
John Dean	---	2	2	---
Andrew Donaldson	---	2	---	---
John Egnew	230	---	---	---
Benjamin Elliot	---	1	2	---
Joshua Elder	100	---	---	---
William Eachens	100	---	---	---
David Edington	100	---	---	---
James Elliot	300	---	---	---
Thomas Edward	300	---	---	---
Daniel Igo	50	2	2	---
John Fee	50	2	2	---
George Fry	300	---	---	---
Ditto	300	---	---	---
Henry Ferguson	100	1	1	---

Barree Township	Acres	Horses	Cattle	Sheep
Thomas Ferguson	100	2	3	---
Ditto	200	2	1	---
Archbald Flatcher	---	2	2	---
Nathaniel Gerard	50	1	2	---
David Gordon	150	---	---	---
John Gamel	400	---	---	---
John Glenn	200	2	2	---
Andrew Glenn	---	2	2	---
Archibald Glenn	---	1	1	---
Benjamin Goffine	---	3	3	---
James Gibson	---	2	3	---
Jacob Hall	300	---	---	---
Abraham Hanes	---	2	---	---
James Kimber	100	---	---	---
Jacob Harmintage	100	2	1	---
George Hutchison	200	2	---	---
Ditto	300	---	---	---
Tho's Holiday	200	---	---	---
Morrison Hance	300	---	---	---
Joseph Hoborn	200	2	2	---
Samuel Hysop	---	3	3	---
Samuel Johnston	100	---	---	---
James Johnston	300	---	---	---
Thomas Johnston	150	2	4	---
William Johnston	200	1	3	---
George Jackson	100	2	3	---
John Kennedy	100	---	---	---
John Kennedy	---	1	1	---
James Kennedy	---	2	3	---
David Kennedy	---	2	3	---
James Kennedy	---	---	1	---
Henry Lloyd	500	4	9	---
James Little	300	3	3	---
William Long	---	3	3	---
John Little	100	2	4	---
William Long, Jun'r	300	---	---	---
Joseph Long	200	---	---	---
Patrick Leonard	100	2	2	---
Joshua Lewis	100	2	3	---
Elizabeth Lewis	---	3	2	---
James McGinnes	100	1	1	---
Jacob Myers	163	2	2	---
John Mitchel	50	2	4	---
David McMoultrie	600	1	---	---
David McGaw	200	---	---	---
Hugh Means	100	---	---	---
David McGaw, dec'd	200	---	---	---
Bartholomew McGuire	80	2	3	---
Means, deceased	200	---	---	---
Alex'r McCormick	300	---	---	---
Ditto	150	5	5	---
William McElvy	300	2	3	---
----- Mifflin	3,800	---	---	---
John Morton	---	2	2	---
Baynton & Wharten	600	---	---	---

Barree Township	Acres	Horses	Cattle	Sheep
Ditto	400	---	---	---
Ditto	500	---	---	---
Ditto	200	---	---	---
William Nelson	200	2	2	---
Abraham Nelson	---	2	2	---
Proprietaries	150	---	---	---
Ditto	700	---	---	---
Joseph Patterson	300	---	---	---
William Fox	200	---	---	---
Joseph Prigmore	250	2	5	---
Samuel Porter	200	---	---	---
William Porter	150	2	3	---
James Patterson	600	---	---	---
William Patterson	200	---	---	---
Ditto	300	---	---	---
Ditto	300	---	---	---
George Reynolds	280	4	4	---
John Reed	250	---	---	---
David Riddle	300	---	---	---
Robert Riddle	300	---	---	---
John Rushe	900	---	---	---
Alex'r Roddy	300	---	---	---
David Ralston	150	2	5	---
Jeremiah Rickets	---	2	2	---
Cheany Rickets	---	2	5	---
Ludwick Sills	100	2	5	---
Ditto	---	---	---	---
Anthony Sills	---	1	2	---
William Smith, D'r	200	---	---	---
Ditto	1,300	---	---	---
Ditto	1,000	---	---	---
Ditto	500	---	---	---
Ditto	200	---	---	---
Ditto	300	---	---	---
Ezekiel Smith	300	---	---	---
John Shaver	50	2	2	---
William Smith, D'r	190	---	---	---
Joshua Skidmore	100	2	2	---
Robert Smith, Esq'r	200	2	1	---
Tho's Shields	150	---	---	---
James Smith	400	---	---	---
John Shea	2,100	---	---	---
Ditto	200	---	---	---
Adam Thompson	100	---	---	---
Benjamin Tue	500	---	---	---
John Taylor	200	---	---	---
Ditto	300	---	---	---
Isaac Thompson	150	---	---	---
Hugh Torbit	100	2	2	---
John Torbit	250	---	---	---
Williams Francis	---	2	3	---
James Thompson	---	2	2	---
John Thorlton	---	1	1	---
Peter Vandivender	80	---	---	---
Samuel Wallace	500	---	---	---

Barree Township	Acres	Horses	Cattle	Sheep
Ditto	100	---	---	---
Williams Wason	150	---	---	---
David Wilson	100	1	3	---
George Wilson	100	1	---	---
Samuel Wallace	400	---	---	---
Thomas Worth	150	---	---	---
John Wilson	200	2	2	---
William Wilson	100	2	3	---
William Watson	---	2	2	---
Isaac Worril	---	2	2	---
Thomas Young	200	5	4	---
Ditto	100	---	---	---
Samuel Ewen	50	2	1	---

Single Freemen

	Acres	Horses	Cattle	Sheep
John Lewis	---	2	---	---
David Lloyd	---	1	---	---
Henry Sullivan	---	---	---	---
Andrew Donald	---	2	---	---
Henry Cannon	---	1	---	---
David Kennedy	---	---	---	---
Peter Craffis	---	---	---	---
William Templeton	---	1	1	---
Robert Spencer	---	1	---	---
David Caldwell	---	1	1	---
Tho's Johnston	---	1	---	---
George Huggun	---	---	---	---
Tho's Long	---	---	---	---
Alexander Ewen	---	---	---	---
James Criswell	---	---	---	---
William Watson	---	1	---	---
John Dean	---	1	---	---

Quemahoning Township

	Acres	Horses	Cattle	Sheep
Casper Stotler	600	6	10	---
Wentle Emmert	230	2	3	---
John Rhoads	200	2	3	---
Joseph Rhoads	200	---	---	---
Jacob Rhoads	150	---	---	---
Michael Sills	300	---	---	---
Jacob Huffman	100	---	---	---
Philip Springer	100	1	1	---
George Kimble	200	2	4	---
John Smith	100	---	---	---
Isaac Miller	---	---	1	---
Ulric Shinglesparriger	100	1	1	---
George Sees	---	---	---	---

Quemahoning Township	Acres	Horses	Cattle	Sheep
David Hully	150	1	2	---
Martin Shutter	200	2	5	---
John Yeoder	150	2	2	---
Peter Reeter	300	---	---	---
Joseph Irwin	200	---	---	---
Ditto	200	---	---	---
Ditto	200	---	---	---
Ditto	200	---	---	---
John Vanderin	300	---	---	---
Ditto	200	---	---	---
Ditto	200	---	---	---
Mathias Mires	200	---	---	---
Elisabeth Hull	200	---	---	---
Edward Higgins	200	---	---	---
Daniel Hoy	150	---	---	---
Barnard Dougherty	300	---	---	---
John Miller	180	---	---	---
John Vander	1,500	---	---	---
James Wells	300	---	---	---
John Reed	300	---	---	---
Thomas McMullen	300	---	---	---
Benjamin Jolley	300	---	---	---
James Boyd	100	---	---	---
Alexander McMullen	150	---	---	---
Richard Brown	300	---	---	---
Hooper and Company	8,100	---	---	---
Christopher Miller	---	1	---	---
Jacob Keever	---	1	---	---
Samuel Wallace	300	---	---	---
John Winsel	150	---	---	---
James Smith	500	---	---	---
Jacob Smooker	200	2	2	---
Solomon Penrod	100	2	---	---
Christian Yeoder	600	2	3	---
Christian Yeoder	---	1	1	---
Simon Shaver	150	---	---	---
Frederick Mostaller	200	---	---	---
George Lower	150	2	1	---
Herman Husbands	400	---	---	---
John Penrod	300	4	4	---
David Right	200	1	---	---
Thomas Vickong	150	---	---	---
James Black	100	4	5	---
Philip Kimble	600	4	6	---
Philip Kimble, Jun'r	100	2	2	---
Christopher Winger	150	---	---	---
Herman Husbands	300	---	---	---
John Peeters	200	---	---	---
John Cable	300	---	---	---

Frankstown Township

	Acres	Horses	Cattle	Sheep
Baynton and Wharton	3,500	---	---	---
Proprietary land, Sinking Valley	16,000	---	---	---
Baynton & Wharton	4,500	---	---	---
Joseph & Edward Shippey	4,000	---	---	---
John Buchannon	600	---	---	---
Gilpen and Comp'y	4,000	---	---	---
Samuel Pleasant	2,000	---	---	---
Alexander Stewart	1,000	---	---	---
Richard Peters	400	---	---	---
William Smith	500	---	---	---
Hugh Means	400	---	---	---
Joseph Donaldson	700	---	---	---
Michael Cryder	1,300	---	---	---
Ditto	300	---	---	---
Cap't Little & William Henry, called Marley Spring	800	---	---	---
----- Cox	1,100	---	---	---
John Armstrong	250	---	---	---
Alex'r Lowrey	397	---	---	---
William Lyon	200	---	---	---
Major Gordon	1,800	---	---	---
Samuel Wallace	1,700	---	---	---
James Hunter	500	---	---	---
Samuel Linsey	500	---	---	---
----- Dickson	400	---	---	---
Cox and Comp'y	7,300	---	---	---
Benjamin Davis	1,700	---	---	---
Cap't Robert Calender	400	---	---	---
Tho's Preter	900	---	---	---
Reuben Hanes	1,800	---	---	---
Widow Gulliford	200	---	---	---
Waugh and Orbison in Comp'y	500	---	---	---
John Gulliford	200	---	---	---
James Holiday	100	---	---	---
John Stevins	50	---	---	---
Joseph Cook	300	---	---	---
Thomas Cook	300	---	---	---
Samuel Davis	300	---	---	---
Michael Wallock	300	---	---	---
Henry Werts	30	---	---	---
James Roddy	300	---	---	---
Henry Werts	100	---	---	---
John Thompson	50	---	---	---
Clark, on Clover creek	100	---	---	---
Parr, on Clover creek	100	---	---	---
Edward Beaty	50	2	2	---
Malcolm Coleman	50	---	---	---
James Carr	45	---	---	---
Matthew Dean	200	2	2	---
Michael Feather	180	3	10	---
Jacob Gripe, Jun'r	50	---	---	---
Daniel Gripe	50	---	---	---
Jacob Gripe, Sen'r	200	---	---	---

Frankstown Township	Acres	Horses	Cattle	Sheep
William Holiday, Sen'r	700	3	6	---
Henry Jarvis	100	---	---	---
William Holiday, Jun'r	50	---	---	---
David Lowrey	300	---	2	---
John Martin	100	---	---	---
John Mortimer	100	---	2	2
Conred Pumpuah	100	---	---	---
William Philips	300	---	---	---
James Spencer	100		1	1
William Seabrooks	30	---	---	---
David Stewart	200	---	---	---
John Stevens	250	---	---	---
Joseph Sellers	200	---	---	---
Philip Stoner	200	---	---	---
Daniel Wollery	400	---	---	---
Jacob Knave, Sen'r	200	---	---	---
Jacob Knave, Jun'r	200	---	---	---
Dutchman Uly	200	---	---	---
----- Butterbaugh	300	---	---	---
Valentine Easter	100	---	---	---
John Houser	200	---	---	---
John Freeman	100	---	---	---
Thomas Coleman	100	---	---	---
John Titus	100	---	---	---
James Crawford	100	---	---	---
Lawrence Swope	100	---	---	---
William Simonton	200	---	2	---
Henry Black	100	---	---	---
Abraham Robison	200	---	---	---
Andrew Divinney	200	---	---	---
Michael Huffnawgle	200	---	---	---
Daniel Moore	300	---	---	---
William Moore	300	---	---	---
Wm. Gulliford	300	---	---	---
Philip Edington	---	1	2	---
Absolam Gray	---	2	3	---
John Hesse	---	---	---	---
James Igoe	---	1	2	---
Joshua Igoe	---	2	2	---
Joseph Miller	---	2	3	---
Tho's Moorehead	---	1	1	---
Godfrey Panther	---	---	---	---
Jacob Roller, Sen'r	---	4	2	---
Jacob Roller, Jun'r	---	4	2	---
Jacob Smith	---	2	2	---
Peter Titus	---	6	3	---
Jonathan Edington	---	1	2	---
Patrick McGuire	---	3	4	---
Aramanus Gray	---	1	1	---
James Johnston	---	2	3	---
John Gorman	---	1	2	---
Joseph Neron	---	1	2	---
Edward Tipton	---	1	2	---
John McGuire	---	2	2	---
Henry Hoshel	---	1	1	---
Edward Bourke	---	2	2	---
Peter O'Reilly	---	2	2	---

BEDFORD COUNTY RETURNS - 1784

Bedford Township

	Acres	Dwellings	Whites	Blacks
James Anderson	260	1	8	--
Thomas Anderson	--	2	4	--
Robert Adams	--	1	6	--
Robert Adams, J'r	--	1	5	--
Solomon Adams	--	1	8	--
James Anderson, J'r	--	1	4	--
William Anderson	--	1	2	--
Joseph Eker	--	1	7	--
John Bonnet	414	1	6	2
George Burket	50	1	6	--
John Black	--	1	6	--
John Bowser	--	2	1	4
Thomas Blackburn	--	--	--	--
William Blair	--	1	1	8
Thomas Burns	70	1	7	--
John Bridges	--	1	7	--
John Crisman	--	1	--	--
Robert Culbertson	200	1	7	--
Lewis Castleman	--	1	9	--
William Clark	100	2	5	--
John Casbeer	--	1	8	--
Henry Crossings	--	1	6	--
Thomas Croyl	--	1	8	--
George Croyl	--	1	8	--
Adam Crice	--	1	6	--
Samuel Davidson	300	1	9	1
Jean Dunlop, widow	--	1	2	--
Michael Dibert	145	1	9	--
James Dunlop	230	1	5	--
James Dalton	230	1	8	--
Samuel Dreenan	--	1	9	--
John Dibert	200	1	7	--
Eleazer Davis	--	1	3	--
Barnard Dougherty, Es'r	360	2	3	--
Ditto, in Friend's cove	200	--	--	--
D'o in d'o	337	--	--	--
Ditto, in Snake Spring Valley	200	--	--	--
Ditto, in ditto	100	--	--	--
Ditto, in ditto	50	--	--	--
Ditto, in Cumberland Valley	300	--	--	--
Ditto, in ditto	150	--	--	--
Ditto, Shawnee Cabbins	267 1/2	--	--	--
Ditto --	171	--	--	--
Ditto --	60	--	--	--
David Espy, Es'r	--	1	5	--
John Etoner	--	--	5	--
George Earnest	--	1	5	--
Valentine Easter	--	1	4	--
Robert Elliot	--	--	5	--
John Ewalt	400	1	5	--
Abraham Evens	--	--	3	--
Peter Easter	100	1	4	--

Bedford Township	Acres	Dwellings	Whites	Blacks
William Elliot	--	1	4	--
David Erwin	--	1	4	--
Frederick Eago	--	1	8	--
James Fleehard	160	1	2	--
Thomas Forker	--	1	5	--
George Fether	--	1	7	--
John Ford	--	1	6	--
Michael Fether, Jr.	--	--	3	--
Michael Fether, S'r	200	1	10	--
Ditto --	170	--	--	--
George Funk	150	1	5	--
Ditto --	125	--	--	--
John Graham	--	1	10	--
Yoast Grant	--	1	4	--
Robert Gibson	--	1	5	--
George Gardner	--	1	8	--
William Gillilan	--	1	9	--
John Gregg	--	1	5	--
Thomas Hays	--	1	2	--
John Hort	--	1	2	--
Dinnis Helm	--	1	5	--
Adley Hemphill	300	1	5	--
William Holiday	--	--	5	1
Elizabeth Henry	150	1	4	--
Christian Houser	--	1	6	--
Frederick Helm	--	1	2	--
John Helm	--	--	5	--
Jacob Helm	--	1	5	--
Patrick Hartford	--	1	5	--
Laurence Her	--	1	2	--
John Johnston	--	1	4	--
Jacob Her	100	1	4	--
George Imler	50	1	7	--
Nicholas Iler	--	1	11	--
Rachel Kenton	150	1	2	--
Thomas Kenton	150	1	3	--
William Kennedy	--	1	5	--
Benjamin Loan	150	1	5	--
Henry Leech	--	--	2	--
John Lafferty	--	1	5	--
Samuel McCashlen, Ju'r	--	1	6	--
Samuel McCashlen, S'r	190	1	9	--
Allen McCombs	139	1	3	--
Cornelius McCauley	300	1	5	--
Arthur McGaughey	--	1	4	--
John McGaughey	--	--	2	--
Duncan McSparran	--	1	7	--
George Milligan	500	1	7	--
Margaret Miller	150	1	12	--
Jacob Miller	--	1	6	--
Jacob Maugh	100	1	7	--
Hector McNeel	--	1	2	--
James McMullen	--	1	7	--
John Mayandrew	--	1	5	--
Frederick Nagle, d'd	200	1	--	--

Bedford Township	Acres	Dwellings	Whites	Blacks
William Neemire	--	1	5	--
Anthony Nawgle	--	1	4	--
George Nixon	--	1	9	--
David Organ	--	1	5	--
William Proctor, Es'r	--	1	10	--
Martin Rieley	--	1	3	--
Timothy Ryan	344	1	3	--
Timothy Ryan	485	--	--	--
Allen Rose	225	1	9	--
William Rose	--	1	2	--
Gabriel Rhoads	100	1	9	--
Frederick Righart	200	1	6	--
George Romach	--	1	2	--
Charles Ruby	--	1	5	--
George Shannon	--	1	2	--
Henry Swager	--	1	8	--
Samuel Skinner	--	1	9	--
Andrew Steel	--	1	5	--
Peter Swopland	--	1	5	--
James Summervail	--	--	2	--
Luke Simpson	--	1	10	--
Rebekah Smith	--	--	2	--
Jacob Saylor	411	1	6	--
William Satorius	--	1	7	--
Daniel Smith	--	1	4	--
William Scovil	--	1	5	--
George Swagart	--	1	3	--
George Sills	160	1	7	--
Adam Samuel	50	1	8	--
Conrod Samuel	150	1	4	--
Peter Stifler	100	1	11	--
Peter Smith	--	1	8	--
Hugh Sampson	--	1	2	--
Michael Sills	100	1	11	--
Ditto	200	--	--	--
John Swagart	--	1	9	--
Matthew Taylor	--	1	2	--
John Todd	--	1	7	--
Edward Taylor	--	1	5	--
William Todd	200	1	6	--
Thomas Vickory	--	1	3	--
Henry Wertz	--	1	8	1
Michael Wallock	--	1	7	--
Philip Wolf	--	1	3	--
James Williams	150	1	6	--
Peter Werts	100	1	8	--
Jacob Willhelm	--	1	6	--
Barabra Walter	100	1	12	--
Rinehart Wolf	--	1	10	--
George Wisecarver	150	1	10	--
George Wertz	--	1	4	--

Bedford Township   Single Freemen

	Acres	Dwellings	Whites	Blacks
John Kenton	150	1	--	--
Thomas McGaughey	100	--	1	--
Single young men without property	--	--	27	--

Non-Residents

	Acres
Doctor William Smith and Company	275
Ditto, on Dunning's Creek	350
Thomas Fitzimmons	350
Ditto, adjoining Andrew Green	450
Andrew Green, adjoining ditto	350
Thomas Drumgold, adjoining ditto	350
Ditto, adjoining ditto	450
William Bradford, adjoining ditto	650
Patrick Wallace, adjoining ditto	500
Ditto, adjoining ditto	500
William Linsey, adjoining ditto	500
Ditto	500
James Mase, adjoining ditto	400
Francis Drumgold, adjoining ditto	350
James Rose, adjoining ditto	450
Ditto adjoining ditto	550
Ditto, adjoining ditto	500
Thomas Atley, adjoining ditto	300
George Shoemaker, adjoining James Rose	600
John Edwards, adjoining	400
James Harvey, adjoining	450
Daniel Clark, adjoining George Shoemaker	450
Joseph Wood, adjoining ditto	500
Ditto, adjoining Colonel Boquet	400
George Mead, adjoining Francis Campbell	350
Ditto, adjoining ditto	399
James Henry, adjoining George Mead	300
James Mease, adjoining ditto	250
Patrick Allison, adjoining James Mease	800
John McMichael, adjoining Alex'r McKee	500
Ditto, adjoining ditto	136
Baynton, Wharton, Morgan & Company	550
Ditto, called Erwin's place	300
Ditto, adjoining Robert Erwin	300
Ditto, called Elliot's place	300
Ditto on Dunning's Creek	200
Ditto, called Francis Campbell's	300
Ditto, adjoining John Flenigan	200
Ditto, ditto	300
Ditto, George Smith	320
Michael Brazill	200
John Finney, adjoining ditto	200
Ditto, in the name of John Frazer	250
George Crohan, adjoining James Harvey	100
Ditto, adjoining Daniel Clark	350

Bedford Township   Non-Residents   Acres

Ditto, adjoining John Ewalt's place	300
Captain Trent and Company	300
Ditto, adjoining Michael Debert's land	300
Ditto, at Lost Run	300
Ditto, Shawney Cabben Waters	300
Robert Evens, adjoining Jacob Harlin's place	200
Joseph Swift, called the Bullock Pens	600
Daniel Clark, on Brush Run	250
William Henry	500
Colonel Boquet, on Dunning's Creek	740
Ditto, Half Way Run	300
Benjamin Chew, adjoining Sill land	600
General Thompson, adjoining Shawney Cabbens	300
Edmond Phisick	160
Levi Andrew Levi, adjoining George Milligan	600
John Pollock, adjoining Elliot's place	600
Ditto, adjoining or near Gregg's place	200
Major Wood, near the Three Springs, now Dr. Smith	300
Ditto, adjoining Dr. Plunket	300
Edmund Miller, near Dunning's Creek	800
George Lancel	150
Elijah Adams	200
John Porter	200
James Gordon	200
Anthony Blackburn	150
William Elliot, Path Valley	180
Peter Easter	300

Colerain Township

	Acres	Dwellings	Whites	Blacks
Isaac Amons	50	1	7	--
Earnest Baker	200	1	4	--
William Baker	--	--	2	--
William Barkley	--	1	4	--
William Beaman	--	--	5	--
Robert Bradshaw, Junior	--	1	3	--
Thomas Bradshaw	--	1	5	--
Robert Bradshaw, Senior	--	1	3	--
David Bradshaw	--	1	3	--
Joseph Bennet	--	1	10	--
Roger Brannen	--	1	6	--
James Barnes	--	1	10	1
David Bell	--	--	5	--
Thomas Beedle	--	--	6	--
Nicholas Crevenston	200	1	8	--
Daniel Collins	100	1	6	--
Charles Cheney	--	1	8	--
Lawrence Coonce	--	1	5	--
Benjamin Cheney	--	1	6	--
Jonathan Cisna	--	--	4	--
John Cisnaa, Es'r	200	--	6	--
Casper Tevebaugh	125	2	9	--

Colerain Township	Acres	Dwellings	Whites	Blacks
Domneck Donely	--	1	7	--
Isaac Denmer	50	--	5	--
Barnard Daugherty, Esq'r	450	--	--	--
Thomas Davis, poor	--	--	1	--
John Daugherty, poor, lame	--	--	1	--
George Elder	--	--	8	--
James England	--	--	5	--
John England	--	--	6	--
John Fleeharty	--	--	10	--
William Frazer	--	--	5	--
Joseph Friend	150	1	8	--
John Friend	180	1	9	--
William Fredregil	--	--	8	--
John Francis	100	--	6	--
William Farmer	--	--	5	--
George Fuback	--	--	3	--
Frederick Hill	--	--	3	--
Thomas Hall	184	--	3	--
Jacob Holtz	--	1	9	--
Patrick Heaney	--	1	6	--
Samuel Hall	--	1	6	--
Elisha Huff	--	--	4	--
John Allem	50	--	9	--
Thomas Allem	--	--	5	--
John Haggan	50	--	7	--
Thomas Hamilton	--	--	7	--
William Jones	--	--	7	--
William James, dec'd	100	--	7	--
Joseph Johnston	90	--	8	--
Thomas Johnston	50	2	3	--
Fergus Regan	--	--	2	--
Nicholas Kegg	--	--	9	--
Robert Love	--	--	6	--
Georg Lightman	--	--	6	--
Robert Moore	450	--	10	--
John McKever	--	--	2	--
Abraham Miley, Shriff	150	--	5	--
Abraham Miley, Junior	150	--	5	--
Samuel Morse	--	--	11	--
Alexander Murphy	--	--	4	--
Daniel Michael	--	--	4	--
Thomas Maghan	--	--	4	--
Nicholas Hain	--	--	3	--
Arthur Ohara	--	--	9	--
James Paterson	--	--	3	--
John Parron, dec'd	62	1	13	--
Mathias Ruff	456	1	6	--
Michael Ruff	--	1	3	--
Nicholas Ruff	--	--	9	--
Peter Ruff	--	--	3	--
John Rienhart	--	1	9	--
Jacob Rolin	--	--	6	--
Rinhart Ripleogl	360	1	10	--
James Rigs	--	--	9	--
Edward Rose	--	--	7	--

Colerain Township

	Acres	Dwellings	Whites	Blacks
James Spurgen	50	--	3	--
Samuel Spurgen	50	1	10	--
Ezekil Spurgen	50	--	8	--
Christoph Tripshoe	--	--	1	--
George Utzler	--	--	1	--
Christopher Utzler	--	--	6	--
Jacob Utzler	--	--	3	--
Henry Williams	--	--	3	--
John Wright, Senior	--	--	5	--
John Wright, Jun'r	--	--	5	--
Benjamin Wigfield	--	--	7	--
Shadric William	25	--	6	--
Henry Whitstone	--	--	6	--
John Willt	50	1	8	--
Ezekil Worley	--	1	1	--
Joseph Wigfield	--	--	12	--
Adam Young	--	--	10	--
Samuel Wickams	--	--	4	--
John William	--	--	9	--
Elizabeth Yeats, poor	--	--	4	--
Joseph Eathenaur	--	--	1	--
Robert Moore, Jun'r	--	--	3	--
Andrew Friend	--	--	3	--
Daniel McMichael	--	--	1	--
George Adamsmous	--	--	1	--
William McDaniel	--	--	5	--

Single Freemen

	Acres	Dwellings	Whites	Blacks
Abraham Miley	125	--	1	--
Ezekiel Worley	150	--	1	--
Jacob Tevebaugh	--	--	1	--
Adam Tevebaugh	--	--	1	--
Andrew Moore	--	--	1	--
James Moore	--	--	1	--
George Utzler	--	--	1	--
Joseph Coughren	--	--	1	--
John Hamilton	--	--	1	--
Henry England	--	--	1	--
James Tucker	--	--	1	--
Lawrence Coonce	--	--	--	--

Non-Residents

	Acres	Dwellings	Whites	Blacks
----- Davis	900	--	--	--
Thomas Hubbs	--	--	--	--
Samuel Davidson	250	--	--	--
Jacob Saylor, Esq'r	250	--	--	--
John Vanderin	300	--	--	--

Colerain Township   Non-Residents

	Acres	Dwellings	Whites	Blacks
----- Galloher	1,200	--	--	--
----- Purvines	400	--	--	--
Hugh Means	400	--	--	--
Samuel Finlay	300	--	--	--
Robert Calender	300	--	--	--
Ruben Heans	400	--	--	--
Thomas Barton	300	--	--	--
Michael Huffnagle	300	--	--	--
David Kenedy	300	--	--	--
Swift and Company	700	--	--	--
Dr. William Smith	250	--	--	--
Samuel Hughes	1,010	--	--	--
William Trent	440	--	--	--
Doctor Allison	250	--	--	--
Samuel Wallace	300	--	--	--
Rowland McDonald	200	--	--	--
Anthony Smith	246	--	--	--
Anthony Worley	50	--	--	--
Thomas Hains	200	--	--	--

Dublin Township

	Acres	Dwellings	Whites	Blacks
Robert Alexander	--	1	--	--
Alexander Blair	--	1	6	--
Benjamin Buird	230	1	5	1
John Buird	50	1	2	--
James Buird	60	1	--	--
Thomas Buird	200	1	3	--
James Barnet	100	1	9	--
Andrew Baringer	--	1	--	--
James Cowan	--	1	6	--
Jean Clements, widow	--	1	5	--
James Coyl, esq'r	263	2	12	--
David Cru, renter	--	--	7	--
George Cunningham	--	--	10	--
David Clark	--	1	4	--
William Craig	--	1	7	--
John Cornelius	--	1	8	--
William Cornelius	--	1	6	--
William Cobran	--	1	6	--
Patrick Cannon	100	1	10	--
Thomas Coal	--	1	1	--
Hugh Davidson	316	1	7	--
Benjamin Elliot	100	--	3	--
Held by Patton	100	1	3	--
Johnathan Edenton	--	1	5	--
John Eagleson	--	1	6	--
Patrick Fitzsimons	--	1	6	--
James Fleming	50	1	8	--

Dublin Township	Acres	Dwellings	Whites	Blacks
John Gallaher	50	1	7	--
William Hutcheson	--	--	2	--
Henry Holt	--	1	9	--
George Hudson	--	1	10	--
William Head	--	1	9	--
William Hunter	--	--	2	--
William Husten	35	1	10	--
Robert Johnston	--	--	7	--
George Lucas	--	1	5	--
James Morton	150	1	5	--
Jonathan Loveall	--	1	7	--
William McDowell	150	--	--	--
Nathan McDowel	150	--	--	--
John Moore	50	1	8	--
James McClewn	70	1	4	--
Alexander McElroy	--	1	7	--
Hugh Mulholam	--	1	4	--
Duncan McDonald	--	1	4	--
James McKee	--	1	4	--
James Marshal	--	1	6	--
James McCord	--	--	7	--
James McBride	--	1	8	--
Philip Mathias	100	1	8	--
Hugh Orlton	--	1	8	--
John Olinger	--	--	6	--
John Pollock	--	1	5	--
Jeremiah Robertson	--	1	4	--
William Ramsey	40	--	10	--
John Ramsey	300	--	--	--
Robert Ramsey	164	1	13	--
John Stitt	--	--	8	--
Thomas Stephens	--	--	8	--
Coonrod Snider	--	--	5	--
James Sheilds	--	--	6	--
Widow Smith	--	--	9	--
David Stiles	--	--	3	--
John Swagart	--	--	3	--
Abraham Suck	--	1	6	--
Mathew Taylor	--	--	7	--
John Tice	--	--	5	--
John Walker	50	1	8	--
William Wilds	--	--	3	--
David Walker	150	1	8	--
Nicholas Welsh	--	--	3	--
John Wilson	--	--	8	--
William Ward	200	1	6	--

Single Freemen

	Acres	Dwellings	Whites	Blacks
Joshua Cornelius	--	--	1	--
Samuel Cornelius	--	--	1	--
William Taylor	--	--	1	--
Simon Kennedy	--	--	1	--

Dublin Township   Single Freemen

	Acres	Dwellings	Whites	Blacks
John Kelly	--	--	1	--
John Morton	--	--	1	--
James Allen	--	--	1	--
Hugh Barclay	--	--	1	--
James Cannon	--	--	1	--
Henry Hyns	--	--	--	1
William Stephens	--	--	1	--
William Willson	--	--	1	--
Thomas Wesoon	--	--	1	--
Thomas Stitt	--	--	1	--

Milford Township

	Acres	Dwellings	Whites	Blacks
Jacob Morningstar	200	--	10	--
Herman Husbands	300	--	--	--
Samuel Wright	--	--	6	--
James Allen	--	--	4	--
Christian Ankeny	346	--	7	--
Peter Ankeny	--	--	7	--
Nicholas Barron	250	--	7	--
Olrick Bruner	300	--	4	--
Henry Bruner	--	--	8	--
George Bruner	--	--	4	--
Jacob Bruner	--	--	3	--
William Baker	--	--	3	--
Rachel Black	--	--	6	--
John Birdman	--	--	5	--
Peter Bugher	--	--	4	1
George Bugher	--	--	2	--
Henry Bender	--	--	2	--
William Bole	--	--	3	--
James Boyd	--	--	--	3
Peter Capp	--	--	--	5
James Claypole	--	--	9	--
James Cooper	--	--	2	--
Christopher Cumm	--	--	4	--
Christopher Cooper	--	--	8	--
William Crichfield	--	--	3	--
William Curry	--	--	7	--
William Kisbeer	--	--	1	5
Joshua Casbeer	--	--	5	--
John Dull	150	--	6	--
John Davis	--	--	6	--
Powel Earnsbarger	--	--	7	--
Adam Fleck	--	--	6	--
Lodwick Fredline	200	--	5	--
James Gilmore	--	--	4	--
Abraham Faith	300	--	3	--
William Hannable	--	--	6	--
John Holle	--	--	9	--

Milford Township	Acres	Dwellings	Whites	Blacks
Charles Hunter	--	--	6	--
George Hunter	--	--	5	--
Jacob Kimel	--	1	4	--
Michael King	--	--	3	--
John Curpeney	--	1	5	--
Jacob Lout	--	1	5	--
Jacob Miller	--	1	6	--
Mary McMichael, widow	--	1	3	--
Hugh Nicholeson	--	1	6	--
Tobias Penrod	--	1	4	--
John Penrod	--	--	8	--
Sarah Parr	--	--	4	--
Francis Philip	--	--	9	--
Adam Hoover	--	--	8	--
Peter Morgan	--	--	3	--
James Noble	--	--	4	--
Alexander Mendair	--	--	5	--
Casper Pile	--	--	9	--
Robert Jones	200	--	4	--
David Jones, Esq'r	--	--	9	--
William Jones	--	--	5	--
George Rise	--	--	5	--
Jacob Sheffer	--	--	4	--
Patrick Sulivan	--	--	4	--
John Shoffe	200	1	7	--
Christopher Swortz	--	--	1	--
Coonrod Vetrich	--	--	5	--
Michael Walter	--	--	5	--
John Weimer	--	--	9	--
James Willson	--	--	7	--
Frederick Wimer	--	--	6	--
Jacob Wimer	--	--	6	--
George Woolf	--	--	4	--
George Wimer	--	--	2	--
James Walker	--	--	2	--
Lodwick Young	--	--	4	--
John Seckman	--	--	5	--

Non-Residents

	Acres	Dwellings	Whites	Blacks
John Sensenig	110	--	--	--
Peter Wanger	150	--	--	--
Jacob Wanger	300	--	--	--
John Rhoads	300	--	--	--
Henry Rhoads	1,200	--	--	--
John Miller	100	--	--	--
George Huck	200	--	--	--
Samuel Pleasant	300	--	--	--
John Mosser	150	--	--	--
Hooper and Company	600	--	--	--
Jacob Roier	150	--	--	--
John Loare	50	--	--	--
Isaac Jones	225	--	--	--

Milford Township   Non-Residents

	Acres	Dwellings	Whites	Blacks
Jacob Ankaney	300	--	--	--
George Funk	200	--	--	--
Mathias Maris	170	--	--	--
Daniel Morningstar	100	--	--	--

Barree Township

	Acres	Dwellings	Whites	Blacks
James Anderson	--	1	9	--
John Armstrong	--	1	5	--
James Cresswell	--	1	6	--
Gilbert Chenney	--	1	12	--
John Cotton	--	1	5	--
Robert Creswell	--	1	1	--
Thomas Ewing	200	1	10	--
John Uing, Junior	--	--	1	--
John Uing, Senior	--	1	5	--
Henry Ferguson	--	1	5	--
Thomas Ferguson	--	1	5	--
John Glenn	--	1	12	--
George Gray	100	1	7	--
Thomas Gray	100	1	4	--
Archibald Glenn	--	1	5	--
Andrew Glenn	--	1	5	--
William Huston	--	--	1	--
William Johnson	300	1	6	--
Patrick Lennon	--	1	10	--
John Litle	--	1	7	--
Hugh Long	--	1	8	--
Thomas Long	--	--	2	--
Joseph Long	--	--	1	--
Hugh Logue	--	1	3	--
William McAlevey	300	1	8	1
Alexander McCormick	400	1	8	--
David McMutrey	1,150	--	--	--
Robert McCartney	256	--	--	--
James McDermott	200	1	7	--
Edward McDermott	--	1	5	--
Benjamin McGavock	--	1	7	--
Richard Miller	--	1	4	--
Abraham Nilson	--	1	4	--
William Nilson	--	1	10	--
Robert Nilson	--	1	2	--
Joseph Oburn	100	1	3	--
William Porter	220	1	6	--
James Porter	--	1	6	--
David Ralston	175	1	10	--
Cheney Rickets	--	1	14	--
Jeremiah Rickets	--	1	4	--
Joseph Reed	--	1	5	--
Robert Riddle	--	--	1	--

Barree Township	Acres	Dwellings	Whites	Blacks
Robert Smith, Es'r	200	1	13	--
Joshua Skedmore	--	1	8	--
David Thompson	--	1	5	--
John Turbert	--	1	4	--
Widow Turbert	--	1	7	--
William Willson	100	1	8	--
John Willson	222	1	8	--
Robert Wason	--	1	7	--
George Willson	--	1	4	--
Thomas Willson	--	1	2	--
Single freemen	--	--	13	--

Non-Residents

	Acres	Dwellings	Whites	Blacks
Thomas Armstrong	300	--	--	--
William Willson, dec'd	180	--	--	--
Ruben Hains	300	--	--	--
Andrew Boggs, deceased	300	--	--	--
John Cox	300	--	--	--
Rachel Cox	300	--	--	--
Robert Carswell	170	--	--	--
John Culbertson	150	--	--	--
Benester and Jiles	600	--	--	--
William Paterson	600	--	--	--
Samuel Miflen	2,800	--	--	--
John Flaxeneer	400	--	--	--
Thomas Rushee	620	--	--	--
John Shea	2,200	--	--	--
The Proprietary	1,500	--	--	--
Baynton, Wharton and Morgan	1,000	--	--	--
John Taylor	150	--	--	--
John Harris	150	--	--	--
William Parks, deceased	200	--	--	--
David Kennedy	400	--	--	--
David Gordon	100	--	--	--
Alexander Roddy	300	--	--	--
George Frey	300	--	--	--
Robert Stevenson	300	--	--	--
Moses Brown	100	--	--	--
James Smith, deceased	400	--	--	--
Samuel Wallace	500	--	--	--
Joseph Shipen	300	--	--	--
James Dickey	100	--	--	--
John Dickey	100	--	--	--
George Hutcheson, deceased	200	--	--	--

Bethel Township

	Acres	Dwellings	Whites	Blacks
Benjamin Abel	100	1	8	--
Adam Ash	--	1	9	--
George Albright	--	1	5	--
Francis Allison	200	--	--	--
Henry Ash	75	1	11	--
John Barley	--	1	7	--
Jacob Brown	--	1	8	--
Henry Bear	--	1	7	--
Edward Breathad	180	1	13	--
David Brown	270	1	6	--
George Bishop	--	1	9	--
Philip Beard	--	1	8	--
John Combs	--	1	10	--
John Curry	--	--	1	--
William Carney	300	1	8	--
John Carney	50	--	1	--
Bethel Covalt	--	1	5	--
Jacob Kegler	--	--	1	--
Edward Combs	--	1	8	--
John Clark	--	1	5	--
Isaac Cowel	--	1	4	--
Thomas Crossens	--	1	3	--
Samuel Crossens	140	1	4	--
Abraham Clevenger	--	1	9	--
Christopher Endslo	260	1	2	--
Widow Eady	--	1	4	--
John Emel	--	1	2	--
John Dart	--	1	7	--
Morris Dishon	300	1	11	--
Timothy Fidler	176	1	11	--
John Fitchpatrick	--	--	4	--
Doras Falmoth	--	1	2	--
John Fisher	253	1	11	--
Daniel Gillan	100	--	2	--
Moses Gordon	--	1	8	--
Morris Gibbins	--	--	1	--
Philip Gibletin	500	1	5	--
Widow Graham	125	1	4	--
Samuel Graves	150	1	6	--
George Powel	--	1	3	--
Martin Hacler	--	1	9	--
James Hollinshead	150	1	4	--
William Hess	--	1	8	--
William Hart	250	1	7	--
George Horse	100	1	7	--
Andrew Hambler	--	1	14	--
Peter Henry	--	1	4	--
Jacob Hendershet	80	1	14	--
John Hill	--	1	2	--
George Hill	300	1	4	--
Jacob Hough	75	--	--	--
Jacob Hakersmith	--	--	1	--
George Hoop	--	1	9	--
George Hawkins	300	--	1	--
William Hunt	149	1	9	--
Balser Hendershald	--	1	7	--

Bethel Township	Acres	Dwellings	Whites	Blacks
George Hoopingarner	--	1	4	--
Ewen Jinkins	284	1	9	--
John Gidion	--	1	4	--
Petter Kimble	--	1	6	--
Robert Kair	100	--	--	--
John Kenard	--	1	4	--
Benjamin Kidd	300	--	--	--
Widow Linn	100	2	5	--
Nicholas Leak	--	1	7	--
James Longstreth	37	1	2	--
John Longstreth	237	1	2	--
Philip Longstreth	200	1	7	--
Martin Longstreth	100	1	8	--
Christopher Lance	--	1	4	--
Isaac Linn	--	1	8	--
Jacob Laman	90	1	10	--
William Latan	--	1	6	--
Samuel Laton	--	1	2	--
George Lamberd	--	--	--	--
Obadiah Laton	--	1	4	--
Asher Laton	--	1	11	--
Andrew Man	340	1	10	--
John Massoon	100	1	10	--
Jacob Mason	--	1	6	--
John Mowney	160	1	6	--
Robert McKenney	75	1	6	--
Joseph McKenney	75	1	3	--
John Milborn	100	1	1	--
James McKenney	262	1	7	--
Barnard Money	125	1	9	--
Edward Martin	--	--	--	--
John Marten	--	--	--	--
Obadiah Malot	--	1	3	--
Benjamin Malot	--	1	5	--
John Macaune	--	1	6	--
Phillip Miller	--	1	8	--
Jacob Maclane	100	1	8	--
James Maclane	--	1	2	--
John Malot, mash	--	--	--	--
Theadras Malot	--	1	5	--
John Malot	--	1	5	--
John Marton	--	1	5	--
Richard Marton	200	1	6	--
James Murry	--	--	6	--
William Marton	300	1	4	--
George Miller	90	--	--	--
Jacob Poorman	100	--	--	--
George Peck	--	1	7	--
Joseph Powel	100	1	9	--
John Peck	--	--	--	--
John Powel	50	--	--	--
Thomas Potteson	200	1	1	--
Richard Pitman	--	1	8	--
William Pitman	100	1	8	--
Moses Reed	--	1	4	--

Bethel Township	Acres	Dwellings	Whites	Blacks
Christopher Raver	150	1	5	--
Abner Roberts	--	1	8	--
Nathanel Rulon	82	1	7	--
Peter Rush	--	1	6	--
Harry Rush, Junior	--	--	--	--
John Rush	--	1	8	--
Henery Rush	--	1	6	--
Jacob Rush, Senior	--	1	3	--
John Smith	--	1	7	--
Adam Smith	123	1	2	--
Peter Smith	186	1	8	--
Lawrence Stiker	113	1	6	--
Elias Stillwell	430	1	4	--
Andrew Seller	--	1	4	--
Henry Snider	--	1	6	--
William Stevens	--	1	4	--
Abednigo Stevens	200	1	5	--
Henery Sowler	--	1	6	--
Hennery Stall	--	--	--	--
John Smith, Licken Creek	94	1	6	--
Hennery Sips	--	1	4	--
Harman Shelar	--	1	5	--
Jacob Shock	--	1	8	--
Tise Shaver	--	--	--	--
Charles Sips	--	1	7	--
Jacob Shingletaker	--	1	7	--
George Shinteltaker	--	1	9	--
Frederick Staub	--	1	8	--
Frederick Swarts	300	1	10	--
Richard Stevens	50	--	--	--
Emanuel Smith, Senior	--	1	1	--
Emanuel Smith, Junior	--	--	4	--
Adam Smith, Junior	--	1	5	--
Thomas Stafford	--	1	9	--
George Swarts	50	--	--	--
William Straight	100	--	--	--
John Slaughter	--	1	2	--
Zachariah Smith	--	1	7	--
Henry Simmerman	--	1	7	--
John Stanely, deceased	--	1	--	--
Mathias Tison	--	1	6	--
Benjamin Truah	--	1	6	--
Samuel Truax	--	1	9	--
Jacob Truax	--	1	11	--
John Truax	--	1	6	--
Joseph Truax	--	1	6	--
Joseph Tharts	--	--	4	--
Stephen Tanner	--	1	5	--
Amos Thachar	--	1	5	--
Connard Watts	--	1	5	--
Thomas Williams	60	1	2	--
Widow Warford	410	1	3	--
Ephraim Wallace	120	1	9	--
Joseph Wilson	--	--	--	--
Francis Welch	--	1	3	--

Bethel Township	Acres	Dwellings	Whites	Blacks
William Wilhelm	--	1	8	--
Jacob Wink	--	1	10	--
William Woods	500	--	--	--
Adam Whorah	--	1	1	--
Widow Walker	--	1	6	--
James Warford	150	1	3	--
Michael Young	--	--	--	--
George Walker	300	--	--	--

Huntingdon Township

	Acres	Dwellings	Whites	Blacks
Samuel Anderson	500	1	7	--
John Ashbough	--	1	9	--
Thomas Armstrong	--	1	3	--
Widow Bower	--	1	6	--
John Biddle	--	1	7	--
Widow Brakenridge	--	1	5	--
Charles Brotherline	--	1	9	--
Jacob Carpenter	--	1	2	--
Michael Baum	--	--	5	--
George Buckhannon	--	1	2	--
James Caldwell	--	1	6	--
Robert Caldwell	300	1	6	--
Charles Caldwell	200	1	6	--
Michael Cryder	--	1	12	--
Peter Craffus	100	1	4	--
Nicholas Craffus	100	--	1	--
Joseph George	--	1	1	--
John Cannon	--	1	5	--
Jacob Canoas	--	1	4	--
Moses Kain	--	1	1	--
Cheney Rickets	--	1	1	--
James Dean	--	--	8	--
Samuel Daniel	67	1	7	--
Peter Dewit	--	3	9	--
John Davis	--	1	7	--
William Dean	--	1	7	--
Benjamin Dreak	--	1	7	--
Thomas Edmoston	--	1	4	--
John Edmoston	--	--	--	--
Benjamin Elliot	80	1	1	--
John Fee, Senior	--	1	3	--
John Fee, J'r	--	1	4	--
Henry Fox	--	1	2	--
Archibald Fletcher	--	1	5	--
James McGinnes	--	1	5	--
Bartely McGuire	--	1	5	--
Thomas Montgomery	--	1	5	--
Samuel Montgomery	--	1	5	--
Nathaniel Gerret, tanner	100	1	6	--
Abraham Heans, blacksmith	--	1	7	--
Jacob Hall	--	1	5	--

Huntingdon Township	Acres	Dwellings	Whites	Blacks
James Armetage	--	1	3	--
Jacob Armetage	80	1	6	--
Samuel Hysop	--	1	3	--
Daniel Egio	75	1	4	1
Thomas Johnson, Senior	150	1	2	--
Thomas Johnson, Junior	100	1	3	--
George Jackson	100	1	13	--
David Kennedy, Senior	--	1	2	--
James Kennedy	--	1	6	--
David Kennedy, Jr.	--	1	1	--
Francis Kennedy	--	1	2	--
Henry Loyd, Es'r	500	2	8	5
Jacob Leard	--	1	6	--
David McMoutry	--	--	--	1
John Mitchel	50	1	4	--
Robert Mitchel	--	--	2	--
John Morton	--	1	6	--
William McElvean	--	1	1	--
John Nearhoff	--	1	6	--
Joseph Prigmore, S'r	--	1	2	--
Joseph Prigmore, J'r	--	1	3	--
Jonathan Prigmore	--	1	2	--
John Patton	--	1	2	--
George Ranalds	280	1	9	--
Edward Rickets	--	1	6	--
Ezekiah Rickets	--	1	6	--
Jacob Roller	--	1	3	--
Anthony Sills	--	1	2	--
John Shaver	--	1	2	--
Solomon Sills	--	1	9	--
Abraham Sills	--	1	6	--
Leonard Swank	--	1	4	--
Lodwick Sills	150	1	6	--
John Spencer	--	1	3	--
Henry Sulivan	--	1	3	--
William Traves	--	1	3	--
James Thompson	--	1	7	--
John Thornton	--	1	6	--
Thomas Thompson	--	1	8	--
Thomas Vaughan	--	1	6	--
John Williams	--	1	8	--
James Williams	--	1	5	--
Isaac Worrel	--	1	5	--
James Willcocks	--	1	4	--
William Wason	100	1	2	--
George Walker	--	1	3	--
Thomas Weston	--	1	4	--
William Watson	--	1	6	--
David Wilson	--	1	5	--
John Young	--	1	5	--
Anthony Johnson	--	1	3	--
James Johnson	300	1	4	--
Samuel Gilespy	--	1	4	--

Huntingdon Township   Non-Residents

	Acres	Dwellings	Whites	Blacks
Samuel Miflin	1,000	--	--	--
John Agnew	150	--	--	--
Joshua Elder	100	--	--	--
William Karr	200	--	--	--
David Eaton	150	--	--	--
Hugh Means	150	--	--	--
John Reed	250	--	--	--
William Eaken	150	--	--	--
Daniel Clark	396	--	--	--
Thomas Smith, Esq'r	900	--	--	--
John Gamble	450	--	--	--
Ezekiel Smith	300	--	--	--
William Johnson	300	--	--	--
Baynton, Wharton & Morgan	1,000	--	--	--
James Dunlap	400	--	--	--
Benjamin Blyth	100	--	--	--
Benjamin Chew	600	--	--	--
John Armstrong	375	--	--	--
Lawyer Johnson	100	--	--	--
Proprietor's land	1,500	--	--	--
D'o	700	--	--	--
Doctor William Smith	3,910	--	--	--
Baynton, Wharton & Morgan	861	--	--	--
Peter Vandevader	85	--	--	--
David Magaw	500	--	--	--
Baynton, Wharton & Morgan	525	--	--	--
John Miner	300	--	--	--

Frankstown Township

	Acres
Widow Gulliford	200
Joseph Cook	300
Thomas Cook	300
Thomas Smith	300
Samuel Davis	300
Michael Wallock	300
Widow Scott	100
James Roddy	300
John Thompson	300
Clark, on Clover Creek	300
Parr, on ditto	300
John Brannon	100
William Holliday, Clearfields	1,900
Asa Brownson	300
Samuel Holiday	300
Adam Holiday	300
John McClelan	300
Thomas McCune	300
Thomas Smith, Esq'r	300
Peter Boyer	100

Frankstown Township   Acres

Michael Faulkener	800
Mathew Dean	300
Michael Fether	189
Jacob Gripes	900
William Holiday, Sen.	700
David Lowrey	300
David Stuart	600
John Stevens	250
Joseph Sellars	300
Daniel Ulery	400
George Butterbough	200
Valentine Easter	480
John Hoser	200
William Holliday, J'r	120
William Simonton	200
Daniel Moore	300
William Moore, Dec'd	300
Baynton, Wharton & Company	4,500
Joseph & Edward Shippen, Chest Valley	4,000
John Buckhanon	600
Gilpen & Company	4,000
Samuel Pleasant	2,000
Alexander Stuart	1,000
Richard Peters	400
Doctor Wm. Smith	300
Hugh Means	400
Donaldson, of York	700
Michael Cryder	1,000
Michael Cryder	300
----- Cox	1,100
William Henry	1,100
John Armstrong	250
Alexander Lowrey	400
William Lyon, Esq'r	200
Major Gordon	1,800
Dixon, on Clover Creek	400
Cox & Company	7,000
Captain Calender	400
Israel Pemberton	190
Cox, on Clover Creek	800
Waugh and Orbison	512
Samuel Wallace	1,700
Captain Litle	100
Cap't Trent & Company	900
Ditto	100
Doctor Wm. Smith	1,400
Captain Wm. Trent	800
Ditto	1,000
Robert Morris	600
Brady & Jones, in Company	15,000
Thomas Vawn	200
Ditto, in Spruce Creek	100
Baynton, Wharton & Company	506
Ditto	512
Ditto, Clear Run	466

Frankstown Township

	Acres
Ditto, Crabb Tree Bottom	461
Ditto	557
Ditto, Walnut Bottom	426
Ditto, Henry Miller	426
Ditto, Shawney Hunting Cabbins	469
Ditto, Long Bottom	679
Ditto, Mountain Run	419
Ditto, on Large Run	343
Ditto, called Mountain Run	445
Ditto, Mulberry Bottom	500
Ditto, called Long Meadows	454
Ditto, called Meadow Ground	427
Ditto, called the Forks of the Indian Path	521
William Dixon	200
Ephraim Blain, at the crossings of Clearfield Creek	300

Sherley Township

	Acres	Dwellings	Whites	Blacks
George Ashman	760	2	7	5
James Armstrong	--	1	3	--
John Armstrong	50	1	2	--
William Adams	--	1	5	--
Daniel Anderson	--	1	5	--
Henry Black	--	1	1	--
Samuel Bell	100	1	3	--
Benjamin Brigges, Senior	--	1	6	--
Benjamin Brigges, Jun'r	100	1	2	--
Samuel Brigges	--	4	4	--
John Boyl	--	1	5	--
James Bratton	--	1	2	--
Charles Boyl	180	1	8	--
George Buckhannon	--	1	3	--
Henry Boyls	--	1	3	--
Henry Burge	220	1	3	--
Thomas Blair	440	1	7	--
Ditto, in Cumberland county	437	--	--	--
William Bryan	--	1	8	--
William Bryan, S'r	--	1	3	--
William Brown, S'r	--	1	5	--
Benjamin Brown	--	1	6	--
William Brown, Ju'r	--	1	4	--
Henry Boyls, Ju'r	--	--	2	--
James Brown	--	1	5	--
James Cannon	--	1	8	--
James Clugage	200	1	8	--
Jacob Crow	--	1	5	--
Andrew Campbell	--	1	3	--
Joseph Campbell	--	1	2	--
Francis Clugage	80	1	7	--
James Conn	--	1	2	--
John Curlet, taylor	--	1	2	--

Sherley Township	Acres	Dwellings	Whites	Blacks
Jacob Cornelius	--	1	5	--
James Crooham, Blacksmith	--	1	4	--
James Carmichael	190	1	9	--
Nicholas Coonce	58	1	7	--
Patrick Caseday	200	1	10	--
William Catham	--	1	3	--
Broad Coal	--	1	6	--
Zachariah Cheney	--	1	4	--
Balser Copenhovan	100	1	6	--
Asiah Davis	--	1	8	--
John Donohew	--	1	8	--
Domnick Damond	--	1	6	--
Joseph Franklin	--	1	6	--
James Fowley	200	1	6	2
James Galbraith	973	1	15	--
Hugh Grim	100	1	4	--
Jacob Grim	--	1	2	--
Jacob Gooshain	--	1	8	--
William Gad	--	--	2	--
George Gooshorn	250	1	3	--
Absalom Gad	--	1	9	--
Even Jinkins	--	1	4	--
Robert Gardner, taylor	--	1	4	--
Joseph Green	--	1	4	--
Even Ginkins, Senior	--	1	3	--
Benjamin Ginkins	--	1	1	--
James Hannah	--	1	2	--
Henry Hardester	--	1	7	--
Nethaniel Hill	--	1	5	--
John Harvey, taylor	--	1	5	--
William Holiday	--	1	6	--
Thomas Hodge	--	1	8	--
Jesse Jeferes	--	1	1	--
John Johnson	--	1	4	--
John Kerr	--	1	9	--
Ditto, in Frankstown	100	--	--	--
Jesse Talkinton, blacksmith	100	1	4	--
George King	--	1	3	--
Thomas Lock	--	1	10	--
Hugh Logan	--	1	11	--
John Latta	--	1	40	--
William Logan	--	1	4	--
James Linn	--	1	6	--
James Love	--	1	1	--
John Luies, schoolmaster	--	--	2	--
James Logan	--	1	7	--
Wilkinson Lain	--	1	8	--
William Long	--	1	5	--
Daniel Lean	--	1	7	--
Samuel Lean	--	1	4	--
Benjamin Long	--	1	5	--
John Love	--	1	6	--
Wm. Maglahalan	--	1	3	--
Andrew Michael	200	1	5	--
James McFeeters	--	1	6	--

Sherley Township	Acres	Dwellings	Whites	Blacks
Thomas Morrow	50	1	9	--
Samuel McMath	--	1	7	--
Thomas Murphy	--	1	4	--
Widow Morrow	--	1	5	--
John Moore	--	1	7	--
Samuel McLaimans	--	1	4	--
William Mason	--	1	6	--
Samuel McCamon	--	1	2	--
John Morgan	--	1	8	--
John Mason	--	1	6	--
Charles Magines	--	1	6	--
James McKrachen	--	1	3	--
Menasah McAleas	--	1	7	--
William Morris	400	1	6	--
Hugh Murrey	--	1	4	--
John Montgomery	--	--	4	--
William Paul	50	1	5	--
John Persons	--	1	2	--
Heathcock Picket	--	1	7	--
Mathew Patton	--	1	5	--
William Patterson	--	1	7	--
Merriman Price	--	1	6	--
Joseph Parish	--	1	4	--
William Polard	2,200	2	10	--
Peter Rieley	--	1	3	--
Jeremiah Rose	--	1	7	--
William Rutter	--	1	4	--
John Rutter	--	1	9	--
Alexander Rutter	--	1	6	--
John Reagh	--	--	2	--
Giles Stephens	--	1	11	--
John Sharaw	100	1	10	--
Adam Stong	--	1	5	--
John Spade	--	1	1	--
William Swan	150	1	5	--
Benjamin Standiford	--	1	4	--
Samuel Stewart	--	1	5	--
Lawrence Swope	--	1	12	--
Jacob Sharow	500	1	4	--
Isaac Sharow	--	1	5	--
John Stevenson	--	1	3	--
James Summervail	50	1	--	--
Casper Smith	--	1	5	--
John Seden	--	1	2	--
John Switzer	--	1	2	--
Benjamin Stevens	--	1	2	--
William Shecklin	--	1	3	--
Sarah Stevens	--	1	2	--
Peter Titus	--	1	8	--
Samuel Taylor	--	1	8	--
John Thompson, S'r	96	1	4	--
David Thompson	--	1	7	--
Samuel Thompson	--	1	9	--
John Thompson	--	1	7	--
Edward Tipton	--	1	5	--

Sherley Township	Acres	Dwellings	Whites	Blacks
John Vantrees	--	1	7	--
James Walcoope	--	1	6	--
William Wiley	150	1	5	--
George Willson	200	1	7	--
Henry Warner	180	1	5	--
Francis Whiteinger	--	1	9	--
John Wain	--	1	1	--
John Wright	--	1	1	--

Single Freemen

	Acres	Dwellings	Whites	Blacks
George Cluggage	900	1	2	--
Robert Clugage, Es'r	155	1	4	--
Ditto, in Huntingdon township	100	--	--	--
Guy Cluggage	50	--	--	--
Thomas Clugage	180	1	1	--
Thomas Clark	--	1	4	--
Robert Galbraith	--	--	1	--
John Gailbraith	--	--	1	--
Samuel Bell	--	--	1	--
John Bell	--	--	1	--
Joshua Coal	--	--	1	--
William Drenan	--	--	1	--

Non-Residents

	Acres
James Berry, Tuscahrorah Valley	100
William Buckhanon, at the mouth of Black Loge creek	300
Minister Duffeld	300
Stephen Duncan	150
John Elliott	200
Samuel Earley	--
Samuel Finlay, near Blair's mill	100
Ditto, near Colonel George Ashman's	200
Harvey Henderson, on the Shade Creek	210
Thomas Hunter, on the branch of Shade Creek	150
Henry Williams	300
James Hunter, on Big Oughwick Creek	200
Ditto, on the Three Spring Creek	100
Samuel Perry	1,100
Baynton, Wharton & Company, known by the name of Red Banks	500
Ditto, known by the name Three Springs	1,300
Christian Kizar	144
William McConnel	200
John Morrison	50
Perrey & Magaw, near Jack's Mountain	260
Ditto, near ditto	200
Ditto	150
John Quigley, Tuscahrorah, Valley	300

Sherley Township   Non-Residents

	Acres
James Reynolds	300
Peter Smith	200
David McMoultry	200
Merchant's land, west of Tuscahrorah	1,100
Ditto, Shugar Run	200
Merchant's land, above the mouth of Black Logg Creek	444
Thomas Mathias, near Shirley old town	440
James Foolan	300
Jeramiah Warder	100
Ditto, held by ditto	250
Ditto, held by ditto	300

Hopewell Township

	Acres	Dwellings	Whites	Blacks
William Abbett	300	1	--	--
Samuel Barrow	600	--	--	--
Andrew Stuart	--	1	1	--
Thomas Buck	--	1	4	--
----- Brannon	100	--	--	--
William Burge	--	1	4	--
Colonel Boquet	1,200	--	--	--
Neal Clark	--	1	1	--
Charles Cann	--	1	2	--
Charles Clark	--	1	7	--
John Covenhoven	--	1	9	--
Company's land	700	--	--	--
Samuel Dean	--	1	1	--
John Dean	--	1	1	--
Thomas Dean	--	1	1	--
William Dean	--	2	11	--
Moses Donaldson	100	1	9	--
William Eyart	270	1	6	--
George Elder	200	1	--	--
John Enyart	--	1	1	--
John Foster	--	2	1	--
James Flora	--	1	2	--
Samuel Finlay	260	--	--	--
Robert Galbraith	1,100	--	--	--
Hugh Guthery	400	1	6	--
Daniel Guthery	--	1	8	--
Henry Hines	--	1	--	--
James Hampson	147	1	8	--
Robert Henry	100	--	--	--
George Heater	--	1	4	--
William Henry	300	--	--	--
John Jinkins	--	1	1	--
----- Johnston	300	--	--	--
Benjamin Kidd	326	1	--	--
----- Keeth	70	1	--	--
Adam Keeth	230	1	--	--

Hopewell Township

	Acres	Dwellings	Whites	Blacks
Richard Lilley	60	--	--	--
John Litle	236	--	--	--
Levi Moore	200	1	3	--
McGaw's heirs	200	--	--	--
Mr. Mitchell	200	--	--	--
Zebulon Moore	50	1	12	--
John Molton	--	1	1	--
James McDonald	--	1	6	--
Michael HuffNagle	150	--	--	--
Ditto	200	--	--	--
Samuel Perry	500	--	--	--
Theodoras Prigmore	--	1	4	--
Edward Rickets	60	--	--	--
William Reed	180	--	--	--
Ephraim Skiles	300	1	--	--
William Smart	100	1	--	--
Sebastine Shope	300	1	--	--
Jacob Shope	--	1	--	--
Philip Stoner	200	1	--	--
Joseph Swift	130	--	--	--
William Sherley	--	1	5	--
Philip Strong	100	1	6	--
John Shaver	200	1	6	--
Saunderses heirs	200	--	--	--
George Sheckley	75	1	1	--
Thomas Smallman	700	--	--	--
Solomon Sills	218	1	3	--
Henry Sheets	--	1	11	--
Samuel Thompson	--	1	6	--
William Wright	250	1	--	--
John White	--	1	--	--
William Watson	--	1	2	--
Michael Whitstone	--	1	--	--
John Weston	200	1	7	--
Zebulon Wilson	80	1	4	--
Thomas Wilson	--	1	--	--

Quemahoning Township

	Acres	Dwellings	Whites	Blacks
Jacob Barnhart	--	1	9	--
Peter Barnhart	--	1	7	--
James Black	--	1	5	1
Israel Burket	--	1	5	--
Christopher Coffman	--	1	2	--
Jacob Clasner	--	1	--	--
Valentine Delabough	300	--	--	--
Thomas Edmon	--	1	5	--
Wentle Emmert	--	1	6	--
George Grose	--	1	3	--
David Holley	200	1	5	--
Jacob Hofman	--	1	3	--
George Hofman	--	1	2	--

Quemahoning Township	Acres	Dwellings	Whites	Blacks
Henry Hess	600	1	6	--
J'r Kimble	--	1	5	--
Philip Kimble, Senior	450	1	6	--
George Kimble	300	1	6	--
Jacob Keffer	--	1	7	--
Michael Kimble	150	1	2	--
George Loar	--	1	7	--
Isaac Miller	145	1	7	--
Christopher Miller	--	1	9	--
Abraham Miller	--	1	8	--
John Miller	--	1	8	--
John Penrod	--	1	4	--
Peter Penrod	--	--	1	5
Solomon Penrod	--	1	6	--
David Penrod	--	1	5	--
John Rhoads	600	1	7	--
James Ross	--	1	7	--
Godfrey Reamon	--	1	7	--
Hugh Robertson	--	1	3	--
Christopher Spiker	200	1	6	--
Casper Stotler	--	1	8	--
Samuel Spiker	--	1	3	--
Jacob Smith	--	1	1	--
Philip Springer	50	1	7	--
Albright Skinglebarge	100	1	2	--
Martin Sooter	300	1	5	--
Michael Sills	200	1	--	--
John Sigler	250	1	7	--
Jacob Smoker	200	1	6	--
Simon Sheffer	--	1	7	--
George Sheck	--	1	3	--
Daniel Stoy	150	1	7	--
Henry Sheffer	--	--	1	--
George Sheffer	--	--	2	--
Philip Sheffer	--	--	2	--
John Ward	--	--	3	--
David Wright	--	1	1	--
John Wensel	--	1	9	--
Michael Whitstone	--	1	3	--
Casper Young	--	1	3	--
John Yother	200	1	7	--
Christopher Yother, Jr.	--	1	4	--
Christopher Yother	600	1	12	--

Single Freemen

	Acres	Dwellings	Whites	Blacks
George Lemon	150	--	1	--
Peter Lemon	150	--	1	--
Christopher Burket	--	--	1	--
William Huskins	--	--	1	--
Jacob Lambert	--	--	1	--
John Smith	--	--	1	--
Christopher Miller	--	--	1	--
George Emmert	--	--	1	--

Quemahoning Township

	Acres
John Vanderin	305
Robert Latis Hooper	302
Daniel Ridehart	301
William Roberts	301
William Robertson	301
Henry Rutter	301
George Rutter	302
George Brown	326
George Lambert	323
John Vanderin	300
John Hunter	324
Andrew McAnear	300
Sacksarel Wood	335
George Jewel	300
Alexander Carlisle	319
Thomas Proctor	372
James Pollock	289
Richard Wells	314
Abraham Digh	307
Benjamin Davis	344
Josiah Harvey	144
Joseph Mather	348
Joseph Morris	302
Joseph Ogden	353
George Hunter	132
John Paul	307
Detrict Reese	308
Thomas Lambert	347
Edward Stell	295
Adam Hubley	328
William Ball	302

Ayr Township

	Acres	Dwellings	Whites	Blacks
Alexander McConnell	--	1	8	--
Adam Linn	--	1	9	--
Amos Stephens	--	1	5	--
Benjamin Williams	--	1	2	--
Barnard Fautt	100	1	8	--
Benjamin Jinkins	--	1	6	--
Ditto, for Erwin	200	1	--	--
Benjamin Peck	--	1	3	--
Benjamin Stephens	--	1	3	--
Bryan Coyl	160	1	3	--
Cathrine Philips	100	1	3	--

Ayr Township	Acres	Dwellings	Whites	Blacks
Charles Taggart	96	1	6	--
Daniel McConnell	400	2	8	--
Daniel McCordy	280	1	5	--
Daniel Royer	435	3	4	--
Daniel Jacobs	200	1	--	--
David Evens	80	1	3	--
David Carlile	--	1	5	5
Daniel Anderson	--	1	5	--
David John	80	1	5	--
Daniel M	--	1	1	--
David Hunter	--	1	5	--
David Erwin	--	1	4	--
Williams Enoch	150	1	5	--
Edward Dorsey	82	--	--	--
Edward Spear	100	--	--	--
Even Shelby	100	1	10	--
Edward Head	150	1	11	1
Edward Graham	150	1	6	--
Francis Shee	--	1	--	--
Frederick Humburd	300	1	16	--
Frederick Myers	--	1	6	--
George Galloway	100	1	4	--
George Sherts	--	1	3	--
George Myars	--	1	4	--
Henry Hoover	200	1	10	--
Henry Davis	50	1	2	--
Henry Chapman	150	1	10	--
Hugh Donaldson	100	1	4	--
Hilley Wilson	100	1	5	--
Hugh Martin	--	1	2	--
Joshua Davis	--	1	9	--
John Hoover	--	1	6	--
John Teat	--	1	4	--
Jacob Poorman	--	1	4	--
Jacob Martin	--	1	5	--
Joseph McKinlay	--	1	6	--
John Willson	270	2	3	--
John Buckley	50	1	6	--
John Scott	210	1	6	--
Jacob John	150	1	8	--
John Anderson	--	1	8	--
James Bella	--	1	4	--
James John	100	1	3	--
John Madden	--	1	6	--
Joseph Bell	--	2	11	--
John Bellman	--	1	6	--
James Gibson	50	2	9	--
John McKinlay	--	2	7	--
James Ramsey	140	1	5	--
John Ranken	140	1	5	--
James Rankin	140	1	2	--
John Kendall	--	1	6	--
James Alexander	--	1	3	--
James Murry	--	1	6	--
John Darby	--	1	3	--

Ayr Township	Acres	Dwellings	Whites	Blacks
John Creadlebaugh	--	1	1	--
James Bell	--	1	6	--
James Simpson	200	1	--	--
John Martin	--	1	1	--
John Linn	--	1	4	--
James Cunningham	200	1	11	--
James McDowell	--	1	3	--
John McClelan	300	2	4	--
James McClelan	140	1	3	--
John McLain	--	1	7	--
John Coleman	--	1	6	--
James Boal	--	1	3	--
John Hammill	--	1	7	--
John Coyle	--	--	1	--
John Oaks	--	1	7	--
John Garry	--	1	5	--
Jean Neasbet	150	1	7	--
Isaac Willson	--	--	1	--
James McConnell	--	1	3	--
James Justice	--	1	3	--
Lewis Davis	100	1	5	--
Lawrence Belzer	--	--	1	--
Margaret Scott	100	1	7	--
Margaret Arthur	--	1	5	--
Mathias Ambrozer	150	1	11	--
Mathias Caldwell	132	1	1	--
Michael Young	--	1	1	--
Nethaniel Hamill	190	1	7	--
Nethaniel Davis	--	1	5	--
Philip Izer	150	1	4	--
Philip Coalman	200	1	10	--
Robert Scott	330	2	2	--
Robert Hamilton	--	1	3	--
Robert Alexander	--	1	5	--
Richard Pittman	95	1	8	--
Robert Hammill	133	1	10	--
Richard Stephens	--	1	4	--
Robert Allen	--	1	6	--
Robert Willson	--	1	5	--
Robert Gibson	--	1	5	--
Samuel Kerr	240	1	8	--
John Sibal	40	1	4	--
Thomas Paxton	150	1	13	--
Thomas John	--	1	6	--
Ditto, for Brown	227	1	--	--
Thomas Willson	--	1	8	--
Thomas Jaques	286	1	--	--
Thomas Lewis	--	1	6	--
Thomas Jackson	--	1	8	--
Thomas Stephens	130	1	7	--
Thomas Davis	100	2	6	--
Thomas Barnett	--	1	6	--
Thomas McCrea	--	1	4	--
Truax Stillwell	130	1	9	--
William Eckles	100	--	--	--

Ayr Township	Acres	Dwellings	Whites	Blacks
Mr. Wood in Maryland	--	1	--	--
William George	100	1	11	--
Wendle Ott	--	1	3	--
William Willson	50	1	5	--
William Patterson	222	1	8	--
William Alexander, Senior	80	1	8	--
William Conner	--	1	2	--
William Alexander, Ju'r	--	1	3	--
William Gibson	--	1	5	--
William Linn	--	1	6	--
William Sloan	210	1	12	--
William Hunter	222	1	9	--
William Gaff	204	1	7	--

Single Freemen

	Acres	Dwellings	Whites	Blacks
Frederick Coon	--	1	6	--
John Mardis	--	1	1	--
Robert Kendall	50	--	1	--
Robert Scott	210	1	1	--
Hugh Alexander	300	1	10	--
Alexander Lowrey	--	1	7	--
John Galloway	150	1	2	--
Thomas Herod	--	1	7	--
Single men without property	--	--	5	--

Brothers Valley Township

	Acres	Dwellings	Whites	Blacks
Frederick Ambroizer	--	1	6	--
Peter Augustine	--	1	5	--
Andrew Bomdrager	--	1	5	--
John Bomdrager	--	1	6	--
Jacob Bowman	--	1	6	--
Stophel Bowman	--	1	6	--
Henry Bittinger	--	1	9	--
Philip Bittinger	--	1	7	--
Michael Beckley	--	1	11	--
Philip Baker	--	1	2	--
Michael Boyar	--	1	5	--
John Berger	--	1	6	--
Joseph Barkdoll	--	1	6	--
John Cresner	--	1	6	--
John Cegy	--	1	7	--
Solomon Claudfelty	--	1	9	--
Frederick Cofman	--	1	2	--
Orn Cressinger	--	1	14	--
Jacob Cefer	--	1	7	--
John Cunts	--	--	13	--
John Cimble	--	1	3	--

Brothers Valley Township	Acres	Dwellings	Whites	Blacks
Abraham Cable	300	1	8	--
Jacob Cable	--	1	10	--
Jacob Caffer	--	1	7	--
Peter Coover	200	1	7	--
George Coalman	250	1	6	--
Nicholas Coalman	100	1	7	--
Nipper Godfrey	200	1	5	--
Casper Durst	200	1	9	--
Henry Davis	70	1	9	--
Valentine Delebaugh	150	1	2	--
David Griffith	500	1	9	--
William Dwire	300	1	2	--
Shaphet Dwire	--	1	3	--
John Etnoyer	--	1	7	--
Joseph Forrey	200	1	7	--
Peter Forrey	100	1	4	--
Henry Fleck	100	1	7	--
Jacob Fleck	50	1	3	--
John Fike	300	1	9	--
Samuel Finlay	100	1	7	--
John Furry	200	1	9	--
Jacob Fisher	300	1	10	--
Nicholas Fouts	150	1	7	--
Ebenezer Grifith	150	1	5	--
Jacob Gibler	100	1	9	--
John Getty	200	1	12	--
Andrew Goodhart	25	1	3	--
Jacob Glasner	200	1	9	--
Henry Glasner	150	1	12	--
Jacob Glasner, Junior	200	--	--	--
John Groner	112	1	5	--
Jacob Good	300	1	4	--
Peter Grave	--	1	5	--
Mathias Gundy	--	1	2	--
Joseph Gundy	--	1	6	--
Christian Gnagey	450	1	10	--
Alexander Hunter	--	1	4	--
James Henderson	--	1	1	--
Christian Hostaler	--	1	6	--
John Hostaler	--	1	4	--
James Hendrix	--	1	6	--
John Hendrix	--	1	6	--
George Hineboch	--	1	6	--
John Hineboch	--	1	5	--
John Hoover	--	1	4	--
Simon Hay	--	1	4	--
Philip Henman	--	1	2	--
John Hiter	--	1	7	--
Christian Hair	--	1	5	--
Felty Hey	--	1	9	--
Walter Hoyle	--	1	8	--
Casper Hoover	--	1	9	--
Adam Hover	--	1	4	--
Jacob Hosteller	--	1	9	--
Clemens Ingle	--	1	5	--

Brothers Valley Township	Acres	Dwellings	Whites	Blacks
Joseph Jones	--	1	4	--
Christian King	--	1	3	--
John King	--	1	7	--
John Laman	--	1	7	--
Peter Livergood	160	1	12	--
Adam Lafaly	--	1	6	--
Benedict Leman, Jun'r	200	1	3	--
Benedict Laman, Senior	--	1	2	--
Peter Laple	100	1	7	--
John Markley	--	1	8	--
Mathias Marker	--	1	7	--
Christian Mast	--	1	7	--
John Miller	--	1	6	--
Peter Miller	--	1	5	--
Jacob Most	--	1	7	--
John Melick	--	1	7	--
George Mathes	--	1	8	--
Michael Miller	--	1	6	--
Christian Miller	--	1	6	--
Frederick Mostoller	--	1	9	--
Joseph Mishler	--	1	11	--
Philip Mathias	150	1	6	--
James McLelan	30	1	3	--
William Miller	--	1	2	--
Henry Marker	--	1	4	--
Philip Mason	--	1	4	--
John Olinger	--	1	7	--
Shrock Oley	--	--	--	--
Lout Valentine	--	1	6	--
Christian Perky	--	1	10	--
Peter Perkey	--	1	6	--
Abraham Perkey	--	--	2	--
Ludwick Pare	--	1	6	--
Ludwick Perkley	--	1	5	--
Elizabeth Plowch	150	1	8	--
Jacob Perkey	N	1	8	--
Adam Pollom	--	1	6	--
Hugh Robison, Senior	--	1	4	--
Hugh Robison, Junior	--	1	5	--
Adam Ringer	--	1	3	--
Yost Sooch	--	1	9	--
John Siller	300	1	11	--
Jacob Siller	200	--	--	--
John Stomm	--	1	5	--
George Rough	--	--	--	--
Leonard Stomm	--	1	6	--
Jacob Stotsman	--	1	2	--
Yost Simmerman	--	1	5	--
Peter Switser	--	1	6	--
Philip Smith	--	1	10	--
George Shenfelt	--	1	8	--
Martin Sooter	--	1	9	--
Coonrod Shaules	--	1	4	--
Boston Shauls	--	1	9	--
Nicholas Sholtz	--	1	5	--

Brothers Valley Township	Acres	Dwellings	Whites	Blacks
George Sweet	--	1	4	--
Jacob Smith	--	1	2	--
Jacob Soock	--	1	5	--
John Switzer	--	1	--	--
Casper Srock	140	1	6	--
Solomon Sheets	--	1	6	--
Michael Sprendiron	--	1	7	--
Joseph Smith	--	--	6	--
Peter Sipes	--	1	4	--
Jacob Snider	--	1	5	--
Frederick Sap	--	1	5	--
William Tice	--	1	6	--
Frederick Tedrick	--	1	3	--
Michael Tryar, S'r	--	1	11	--
Michael Tryar, J'r	--	1	6	--
Yost Teets	--	1	4	--
John Tryar	--	1	3	--
Christian Tryar	--	1	3	--
Widow Walker	--	1	7	2
Peter Winger	--	1	6	--
Jacob Winger	300	1	6	--
Philip Wegley	--	1	7	--
Isaac Yowler	--	1	9	--
John Yoder	--	1	6	--
Andrew Baker	--	--	1	--
John Bowman	--	--	1	--
John Brent	--	--	1	--
Abraham Craft	--	1	1	--
Christian Fike	--	1	1	--
John Ferguson	--	--	1	--
John Griffith	--	--	1	--
Jacob Markley	200	1	1	--
George Shackley	--	--	1	--
Ludwick Sheets	--	--	1	--
John Tederick	--	--	1	--
Daniel Mickey	--	--	1	--
Christian Toder	--	--	1	--
John Vanderin	300	--	1	--
Henry Baker	200	--	--	--
Peter Adams	200	--	--	--
John Glass	200	--	--	--
Eli Brier	300	--	--	--
Christian Stoner	112	--	--	--
Stephen Tanner	200	--	--	--
John Vanderin	300	--	--	--
Ditto	300	--	--	--
George Shaver	300	--	--	--
Mr. Frey	200	--	--	--
Mathias Maris	100	--	--	--
Frederick Nawgle, dec'd	50	--	--	--
John Vanderin	600	1	--	--
Mr. Ewin	300	1	--	--
John Hood	600	1	--	--
Jacob Good	270	1	--	--
John Yoder	200	--	--	--

Brothers Valley Township	Acres	Dwellings	Whites	Blacks
Thomas Smith	300	--	--	--
Benjamin Chue	300	1	--	--
Ditto, held by d'o	600	--	--	--
Cox & Company	260	--	--	--
Benjamin Chue	300	--	--	--
Ditto	300	--	--	--
Ditto	200	--	--	--
Ditto held by d'o	250	--	--	--
Ditto by ditto	500	--	--	--
Ditto, by ditto	900	--	--	--
John Stump	500	1	--	--

Providence Township

	Acres	Dwellings	Whites	Blacks
John Moore	1,000	1	7	--
Francis South	--	1	3	--
William Ervin	50	1	2	--
Joseph Morrison	200	1	5	--
Henry Armstrong	--	1	4	--
William Waugh	--	--	2	--
John Gibson	150	1	3	--
Hugh Ferguison	100	1	6	--
John Ferguison	200	--	3	--
John Mortimer	--	--	3	--
Samuel Moore	150	1	6	--
Benjamin Elliot	272	1	4	--
Henry Livingston	--	--	5	--
John Elliot	--	1	6	--
John Paxton	300	--	6	--
Daniel McKarty	--	--	3	--
John Richey	480	--	6	--
Thomas Woods	246	1	9	--
John Livingston	--	--	8	--
Robert Williams	--	--	7	--
Henry Devee	--	1	5	--
William Boyd	--	1	6	--
John Shaver	238	1	7	--
John Boyd	--	--	4	--
Daniel Means	--	--	4	--
George Enslow	--	1	4	--
James Martin, Es'r	125	1	9	1
Martin Kersman	--	--	6	--
Joseph Commins	--	1	6	--
David Smith	--	1	9	--
Joseph Sparks	--	--	3	--
Mathias Hollard	100	1	3	--
Henry Hollard	--	--	2	--
John Stackman	--	--	2	--
Thomas Pennal	--	--	1	--
Joseph Chapman	--	--	6	--
William McDonald	--	--	4	--
Adam Wimmer	--	--	6	--

Providence Township	Acres	Dwellings	Whites	Blacks
John Wimmer	--	--	2	--
John Shaver, Junior	--	--	6	--
John Smith	--	--	2	--
Isaac Wimer	--	1	6	--
Cathrine Zantlinger	--	--	6	--
Mathias Swartzwell	--	--	10	--
Uriah Blyew	--	--	1	--
Cornelius Seamans	--	--	3	--
Jacob Weyley	--	--	2	--
Edward Donalds	--	--	8	--
Andrew Jones	--	--	2	--
Abiah Akers	--	--	5	--
Jonathan Buck	--	--	5	--
Thomas Norton	--	--	3	--
John McKinney	--	--	9	--
Andrew Blackhart	--	--	3	--
John Williams	--	--	9	--
John Piper	300	1	7	--
Joseph McFarren	--	--	4	--
Richard Kimber	--	--	2	--
Jacob Miller	--	--	2	--
Henry Hinish	--	1	7	--
Mathias Myars	--	--	4	--
Adam Miller	--	--	8	--
James Applegate	--	--	2	--
James French	--	1	10	--
John Morehead	--	--	1	--
Abraham Covalt	--	1	10	--
John Peck	--	--	3	--
George May	--	--	3	--
Amos Jones	--	1	4	--
John Cravens	--	--	4	--
Widow McDonald	--	--	6	--
Joseph McDonald	188	1	5	--
Keenan Rowland	--	--	2	--
Thomas Megibens	--	--	2	--

Single Freemen

	Acres	Dwellings	Whites	Blacks
William Gibson	150	--	4	--
Francis Reynolds	50	--	2	--
John McLamins	250	--	4	--
David Buck	--	--	4	--
George Enslow	--	--	1	--
James Smith	--	--	1	--
James Mortimer	--	--	1	--
John Bays	--	--	1	--
Peter Oneal	--	--	1	--
Ephraim Akers	--	--	1	--
Thomas Earnest	--	--	1	--
William Boyd	--	--	1	--
Nicholas Shaver	--	--	1	--
Robert Moore	100	--	--	--
John Cessna	100	--	--	--
John Allison	150	--	--	--

Providence Township   Single Freemen

	Acres	Dwellings	Whites	Blacks
John Ormsby	369	1	--	--
Henry Waldren	300	--	--	--
John Breathod	200	--	--	--
Peter Smith	170	--	--	--
James Hunter	600	--	--	--
John Allison	204	--	--	--
Edward Elliot	1,100	--	--	--
Donalson, of York	1,400	--	--	--
George Elder	400	--	--	--
George Nixon	200	--	--	--
Charles Cox	300	--	--	--
Barnard Daugherty	367	--	--	--

Cumberland Valley Township

	Acres	Dwellings	Whites	Blacks
James Arnet	215	1	8	--
Jacob Aswalt	50	4	3	--
Tobias Aswalt	--	1	3	--
Anthony Asher	--	1	6	--
Samuel Arnold	--	1	1	--
John Albright	--	1	6	--
George Amarine	--	1	3	--
Henry Amrine	--	1	5	--
Abraham Amrine	--	1	1	--
Nethaniel Burdue	--	1	5	--
Patrick Burnes	300		5	--
Thomas Boyd	--	1	9	--
Valentine Baker	--	1	3	--
Thomas Blackburn	--	1	4	--
John Blyew	--	1	5	--
Joseph Buck	300	1	1	--
Richard Baker	--	1	1	--
George Baker	--	1	6	--
Andrew Borland	125	1	3	--
Samuel Borland	125	1	2	--
John Buck	--	1	4	--
Thomas Blair	100	1	4	--
Bryce Blair	100	1	4	--
William Bell	--	1	4	--
Jacob Bowser	--	1	1	--
Peter Buzzard	--	1	4	--
William Browning	--	1	4	--
Robert Campbell	150	1	3	--
John Cisna, Esq'r	100	1	3	--
Charles Cissna	300	1	10	1
Thomas Casteel	--	1	3	--
William Cowan	--	1	3	--
Thomas Conoway	580	1	2	--
Thomas Coulter	--	1	10	--

Cumberland Valley Township	Acres	Dwellings	Whites	Blacks
Christopher Cruey	--	1	8	--
George Cook	--	1	1	--
James Crossbey	--	1	6	--
Patrick Cavaner	--	1	4	--
Shaderick Casteel		1	3	--
Even Cissna	150	1	7	--
Richard Croy	--	1	5	--
Jacob Croy	--	1	3	--
Jonathan Cessna	170	--	--	--
Michael Cofman	--	1	1	--
Cornelius Devour	127	1	7	--
Ezedekiah Duckman	100	1	7	--
Luke Devour	--	1	5	--
Thomas Dickenson	--	1	8	--
Amos Dickenson	--	1	5	--
Michael Dughman	--	1	2	--
John Dughman	--	1	3	--
Christian Dughman	150	1	7	--
Daniel Devoure	--	1	1	--
William Devoure	--	1	5	--
Stephen Dickinson	--	1	1	--
John Elder	100	1	6	--
Gerrett Evens	--	1	3	--
Thomas Faris	200	1	3	--
Jacob Fox	150	1	6	--
John Farmer	--	1	9	--
Martin Feats	--	1	7	--
John Feats	--	1	3	--
George Feats	--	1	1	--
George Funk	100	--	--	--
Samuel Finlay	--	1	3	--
Moses Gooden	--	1	7	--
Aaron Gooden	--	1	5	--
John Haines, Esq'r	133	1	4	--
Andrew Hudson	--	1	9	--
Robert Huston	--	1	2	--
Edward Huston	--	1	1	--
Alexander Huston	--	1	9	--
Tobias Hogland	--	1	1	--
Philip Hogar	--	1	9	--
John Iems	28	1	3	--
Joseph Kelly	319	1	7	--
Mathew Kelly	--	1	5	--
Adam Kuzer	--	1	3	--
John Lazer, Junior	--	1	7	--
Richard Low	--	1	6	--
Thomas Lazer	--	1	8	--
John Lazer	--	1	3	--
Joseph Lazer	--	1	6	--
Henry Laine	--	1	1	--
George Lebarger	100	1	5	--
Ludwick Lebarger	--	1	6	--
Nicholas Lebarigar	100	1	7	--
Joseph Liddy	--	1	6	--
Lawrence Lambe	--	1	1	--

Cumberland Valley Township	Acres	Dwellings	Whites	Blacks
Timothy Lambe	---	1	4	---
John Lambe	---	1	2	---
Henry Michael	---	1	7	---
William Masters	6	1	1	---
Paul Michael	---	1	2	---
Cristman Nice	---	1	8	---
John Neemire	---	1	3	---
Jacob Neemire	---	1	3	---
Peter Neemire	---	1	1	---
Jonathan Potts	50	1	3	---
William Purdue, J'r	50	1	3	---
William Purdue, S'r	200	1	7	---
Samuel Paxton	---	1	7	---
John Porton	---	1	7	---
Daniel Proser	---	1	3	---
John Parker	---	1	9	---
Isaac Plummer	---	1	11	---
Thomas Rhea	---	1	9	---
Jacob Rice	---	1	4	---
Jacob Rhoads	---	1	6	---
Frederick Rice	50	1	7	---
Joseph Rhoads	---	1	3	---
Peter Sheckley	---	---	1	---
John Switzer	---	1	2	---
Nathaniel Screechfield	---	1	3	---
John Schreechfield	---	1	2	---
Andrew Sherer	---	1	7	---
Mathias Sheets	---	1	1	---
John Spurgen	---	1	3	---
George Squires	---	1	2	---
Nathaniel Screechfield, S'r	---	1	4	---
Benjamin Schreechfield	---	1	5	---
John Sempleton	---	1	6	---
Frederick Sever	---	1	8	---
John Turner	---	1	4	---
Jacob Tarwater	---	1	3	---
John Tumbleston	170	1	8	---
Benjamin Tumbleston	200	---	---	---
Henry Tumbleston	---	1	2	---
Jacob Valentine	---	1	7	---
Philip Warnief	50	1	8	---
Robert Wadsworth	---	1	3	---
William Workman	---	1	4	---
Powel Wilker	---	1	3	---
Godfrey Woolbach	---	1	7	---
George Willhelm	---	1	2	---
Alexander Willhelm	---	1	2	---
Andrew Wilker	---	1	4	---
Joseph Workman	---	1	2	---
Edward Warran	---	1	6	---
Thomas Wood	---	1	6	---
David Walter	---	1	3	---
James Young	---	1	3	---
William Young	---	1	2	---
Robert Lusk	250	---	---	---

Cumberland Valley Township	Acres	Dwellings	Whites	Blacks
Edward Ward	75	--	--	--
Samuel Finlay	500	--	--	--
Samuel Perry	200	--	--	--
David Sample	265	--	--	--
Richard Peters	1,050	--	--	--
Andrew Steel	225	--	--	--
Richard Dunlap, deceased	250	--	--	--
John Galaher	150	--	--	--
William Thompson, deceased	300	--	--	--
George Campbell & Company	1,000	--	--	--
Ralph Snider	200	--	--	--
Captain Baset	400	--	--	--
James Scott	300	--	--	--
Baynton, Wharton and Company	1,000	--	--	--
Colonel Robert Morris and the Rev'd Thomas White, formerly Doctor Smith	900	--	--	--
Richard Peeters, Es'r	193	--	--	--
Ditto	133	--	--	--
Ditto	218	--	--	--
Ditto	302	--	--	--
Ditto	180	--	--	--
Ditto	223	--	--	--
Ditto	211	--	--	--
Ditto	300	--	--	--

INDEX

Titles, positions, jr. and sr. were omitted. Placenames which implied family names were used. Thus, "Smith's land" would appear in the index as "SMITH -----". The spelling of names was not altered from that found in the published Pennyslvania Archives.

The Publisher

ABBETT, William 59
ABEL, Benjamin 48
ABIT, Benjamin 19
ABRAHAM, Gabriel 5
   Thomas 6
ABRAHAMS, Henry 5
ADAM, Peter 8
ADAMS, Elijah 1, 39
   Jacob 17
   Peter 68
   Robert 1, 35
   Solomon 1, 35
   William 55
ADAMSMOUS, George 41
AGNEW, John 53
AKERS, Abiah 70
   Ephraim 70
ALBRIGHT, George 48
   John 71
ALBUGH, Frederic 28
ALEXANDER, Alexander 17
   Hugh 65
   James 6, 17, 63
   Robert 17, 42, 64
   William 17, 65
ALLEM, John 40
   Thomas 40
ALLEN, James 44
   Robert 17, 64
   Widow 6
ALLFATER, Frederick 8
ALLISON, Doctor 42
   Francis 23, 48
   John 16, 70, 71
   Patrick 38
ALMS, John 12
   Thomas 12
AMARINE, George 71
AMBROIZER, Frederick 65
AMBROSIA, Frederick 8
   Mathias 17
AMBROZER, Mathias 64
AMIL, John 19
AMONS, Isaac 13, 39
AMRINE, Abraham 71
   George 12
   Henry 12, 71

ANDERSON, Alexander 24
   Daniel 17, 24, 55, 63
   James 1, 35, 46
   John 17, 63
   Samuel 28, 51
   Stewart 14
   Thomas 1, 35
   William 16, 35
ANDRIS, William 19
ANKANEY, Jacob 46
ANKENY, Christian 44
   Christopher 6
   Peter 6, 44
APPLEBY, John 24
APPLEGATE, James 70
ARMETAGE, Jacob 52
   James 52
ARMSTRONG, Eleanor 24
   George 27
   Henry 69
   James 55
   John 27, 28, 33, 46, 53, 54, 55
   Thomas 17, 47, 51
ARNET, James 71
   Thomas 13, 14
   William 15
ARNOLD, Samuel 71
ARTHUR, Hope 28
   Margaret 17, 64
ARTT, William 19
ASH, Adam 19, 48
   Henry 48
ASHBOUGH, John 51
ASHER, Anthony 71
ASHERS, Anthony 3
ASHMAN, George 24, 55, 58
ASWALT, Jacob 3, 71
   Tobias 71
ATLEY, Thomas 38
AUGUSTIN, Peter 8
AUGUSTINE, Peter 65

BAIR, Michael 8
BAKER, Andrew 11, 68
   Earnest 13, 39

   George 71
   Henry 68
   Philip 8, 65
   Richard 71
   Samuel 27
   Valentine 71
   William 39, 44
BALL, David 13
   William 62
BARCLAY, Hugh 44
BARINGER, Andrew 42
BARKDOLL, Joseph 65
BARKER, James 8
BARKEY, Christian 8
BARKLEY, Ludwick 8
   William 39
BARLEY, John 48
BARN, James 12
BARNES, James 39
BARNET, James 42
   Thomas 17
BARNETT, James 24
   Thomas 64
BARNHART, Jacob 60
   Peter 60
BARNINGER, Andrew 24
BARRMAN, Jacob 19
BARRON, Nicholas 44
BARROW, Samuel 59
BARTHOLOMEW, Roharty 17
BARTON, Thomas 42
BASET, Captain 74
BAUGH, Leonard 17
BAUM, Michael 51
BAWSER, John 28
BAYARD, John 1
BAYNTON, ----- 16, 27, 29, 30, 33, 38, 47, 53, 54, 55, 58, 74
BAYS, John 70
BEAMAN, William 39
BEAMER, William 12
BEAR, Henry 48
BEARD, Philip 48
BEATTY, James 1
BEATY, Edward 33
BEAVEN, John 12

INDEX

BECKLEY, Michael 65
BEDINGER, Henry 8
  Philip 8
BEEDLE, Thomas 39
BEEGHLEY, Michael 8
BELL, David 39
  James 17, 64
  John 24, 27, 58
  Joseph 17, 63
  Samuel 24, 55, 58
  William 3, 71
BELLA, James 63
BELLMAN, John 63
BELZER, Lawrence 64
BENDER, Henry 44
BENESTER, ----- 47
BENFORD, John 8
BENNET, Joseph 39
  William 14
BENNIT, Joseph 12
BENSENT, ----- 28
BERGER, John 65
BERKEY, Jacob 8
  John 8
BERNHART, Jacob 6
BERRY, James 58
BIDDLE, John 51
  Thomas 13
BILLIEU, John 3
BIRD, James 24
  Thomas 24
BIRDMAN, John 44
BISHOP, George 19, 48
  Jonathan 3
BITTINGER, Henry 65
  Philip 65
BLACK, Henry 34, 55
  James 32, 60
  John 35
  Rachel 44
  William 6
BLACKBURN, Anthony 39
  Thomas 1, 35, 71
BLACKHART, Andrew 70
BLAIN, Ephraim 55
BLAIR, ----- 58
  Alexander 24, 42
  Bryce 3, 71
  Thomas 24, 27, 55, 71
  William 1, 35
BLOWITH, White 8
BLYEW, John 71
  Uriah 70
BLYTH, Benjamin 28, 53
BOAL, James 64

BOGGS, Andrew 47
BOLE, William 44
BOMDRAGER, Andrew 65
  John 65
BONNET, John 1, 35
BOOGER, Abraham 11
  John 8
  Peter 8
BOOHER, Peter 6
BOOKER, Samuel 11
BOQUET, Colonel 16, 38, 39, 59
BORELAND, Andrew 3
  Samuel 5
BORLAND, Andrew 71
  Samuel 71
BORNDRAGER, John 8
BOUQUET, Colonel 28
BOURKE, Edward 34
  George 6
BOWER, Widow 51
BOWMAN, Jacob 8, 65
  John 11, 68
  Stophel 8, 65
BOWSER, Jacob 71
  John 1, 35
BOYAR, Michael 65
BOYD, James 6, 32, 44
  John 13, 69
  Thomas 3, 71
  William 13, 69, 70
BOYER, Peter 53
BOYL, Charles 24, 55
  John 55
BOYLS, Henry 24, 55
BRADFORD, William 38
BRADSHAW, David 39
  Robert 13, 39
  Thomas 13, 39
BRADY, ----- 54
BRAKENRIGDE, Widow 51
BRANNEN, Roger 39
BRANNON, ----- 59
  John 53
BRATTON, James 55
BRAZILL, Michael 38
BREADY, John 28
BREATHAD, Edward 48
BREATHED, John 19
BREATHOD, John 71
BRENT, John 68
BRIDENBURGH, Abraham 8
BRIDGES, James 15
  John 13, 35
BRIER, Eli 68

BRIGGES, Benjamin 55
  Samuel 55
BRIGGS, Benjamin 24
  Samuel 24
BRIGHT, Peter 11
BRIGHTS, George 8
BRINGHURST, James 23
BROOKENS, Charles 1
BROTHERLINE, Charles 51
BROTHERS, Francis 24
BROTHERTON, Charles 28
BROWN, ----- 64
  Benjamin 24, 55
  David 19, 48
  George 62
  Henry 6
  Jacob 19, 48
  James 17, 55
  Moses 47
  Richard 32
  Thomas 19
  William 24, 55
BROWNING, William 3, 71
BROWNSON, Asa 53
BRUNER, George 6, 44
  Henry 6, 44
  Jacob 44
  Olrick 44
  Ulric 6
BRUSER, Henry 19
BRUSH, ----- 39
BRYAN, William 24, 55
BUCHANNEN, William 27
BUCHANNON, John 33
BUCK, David 13, 70
  John 11, 71
  Jonathan 70
  Joseph 71
  Thomas 16, 59
BUCKHANNON, George 51, 55
BUCKHANNON, John 54
  William 58
BUCKLEY, John 17, 63
BUGHER, George 44
  Peter 44
BUIRD, Benjamin 42
  James 42
  John 42
  Thomas 42
BUNN, William 16
BUNNS, William 28
BURD, Benjamin 24
  John 19, 24
BURDUE, Nethaniel 71
BURG, Henry 24

INDEX

BURGE, Henry 55
  William 59
BURKET, Christopher 61
  George 35
  Israel 60
BURKETT, George 1
BURNES, Patrick 71
BURNS, Patrick 3
  Thomas 11, 35
BUSH, Christofer 19
BUTTERBAUGH, ----- 34
BUTTERBOUGH, George 54
BUZZARD, Peter 3, 71
BYSER, William 14

CABEL, Jacob 8
  Philip 8
CABLE, Abraham 6, 66
  Jacob 66
  John 32
CAFFER, Jacob 66
CAHEL, Abram 8
CALDWELL, Charles 28, 51
  David 31
  James 51
  Mathias 64
  Matthew 17
  Robert 28, 51
CALENDER, Captain 54
  Robert 33, 42
CAMP, Hercules 24
CAMPBEL, Robert 3
CAMPBELL, Andrew 55
  Collin 17
  Dougal 17
  Dougall 23
  Francis 38
  George 74
  Joseph 55
  Robert 19, 71
CANN, Charles 59
CANNON, Henry 31
  James 27, 44, 55
  John 28, 51
  Patrick 24, 42
CANOAS, Jacob 51
CANON, James 24
CANOR, Jacob 28
CANOTE, Henry 24
CAPP, Peter 44
CARLILE, David 17, 63
CARLISLE, Alexander 62
CARMICHAEL, James 24, 56
CARNEY, John 48
  William 23, 48

CARPENTER, Daniel 28
  Jacob 51
CARR, James 33
  William 28
CARRS, Widow 19
CARSWELL, Robert 47
CARTER, Thomas 27
  William 27
CASBEER, John 35
  Joshua 44
CASEDAY, Patrick 56
CASSEDY, Patrick 24
CASTEEL, Shaderick 72
  Shadrach 3
  Thomas 3, 71
  Zadock 5
CASTLEMAN, Lewis 35
CATHAM, William 56
CAVANER, Patrick 72
CEFER, Jacob 65
CEGY, John 65
CEMAN, Cornelius 14
  Isaac 13
CESNA, Charles 3
  Evan 3
  John 3, 13
  Jonathan 1, 5, 13
  Joseph 3
CESSNA, John 70
  Jonathan 72
CHAPMAN, Henry 17, 63
  Joseph 12, 69
CHARLETON, Samuel 24
CHENEY, Benjamin 39
  Charles 39
  Zachariah 56
CHENNEY, Gilbert 46
CHERRY, Benjamin 16
CHEST, ----- 54
CHEW, Benjamin 39, 53
CHILCOT, Robison 24
CHRISTNER, John 8
CHUE, Benjamin 69
CIMBLE, John 65
CISNA, John 71
  Jonathan 39
CISNAA, John 39
CISSNA, Charles 71
  Even 72
CLARK, ----- 33, 53
  Charles 15, 59
  Daniel, 28, 38, 39, 53
  David 42
  John 48

  Neal 59
  Neil 15
  Thomas 27, 58
  William 1, 35
CLASNER, Jacob 60
CLAUDFELTY, Solomon 65
CLAYPOLE, James 44
CLAYTON, Daniel 16
CLEARFIELD, ----- 55
CLEMEN, William 14
CLEMENTS, Jean 42
CLEVENGER, Abraham 48
CLEVINGER, Abraham 19
CLUGAGE, Francis 28, 55
  Gaven 27
  Gavin 24
  George 24, 27
  James 24, 55
  Robert 58
  Thomas 58
CLUGGAGE, George 58
  Guy 58
COAL, Broad 24, 56
  Joshua 58
  Thomas 42
COALMAN, George 66
  Nicholas 66
  Philip 64
COBEL, Joseph 19
COBRAN, William 42
COFFMAN, Christopher 60
  Frederick 11
COFMAN, Frederick 65
  Michael 72
COLE, Thomas 24
COLEMAN, George 8
  John 8, 64
  Malcolm 33
  Nicholas 8
  Thomas 34
COLLINS, Daniel 12, 39
COMBS, Edward 19, 48
  John 48
COMMINS, Joseph 69
COMPANY, ----- 59
COMPTON, James 3
COND, James 24
CONN, James 55
CONNER, Edward 17
  William 17, 65
CONOWAY, Thomas 71
COOK, George 72
  Joseph 33, 53
  Thomas 33, 53
COOMBS, John 23

77

INDEX

COON, Frederick 65
COONCE, Lawrence 39, 41
  Nicholas 56
COONS, Laurence 13
COONTS, Nicholas 24
COONTZ, Lawrence 14
COOPER, Christopher 8, 44
  James 44
COOVER, Peter 66
COPENHAVER, Batzer 24
COPENHOVAN, Balser 56
CORNELIUS, Jacob 56
  John 24, 42
  Joseph 24
  Joshua 43
  Samuel 43
  William 24, 42
COTTON, John 46
COUGHREN, Joseph 41
COULTER, Thomas 3, 71
COUNTRYMAN, ----- 8
  George 6
COUNTY, Joseph 8
COVALT, Abraham 13, 70
  Bethel 48
  Bethuel 22
COVENHOVEN, John 59
COVINHOVEN, John 15
COWAN, James 42
  William 71
COWEL, Isaac 48
COWEN, William 1
COWL, Abraham 23
COX, ----- 5, 33, 54, 69
  Charles 71
  John 28, 47
  Rachel 28, 47
  William 8
COYL, Bryan 17, 62
  James 24, 42
  John 17
COYLE, John 64
CRABB TREE, ----- 55
CRAFFACE, Nicholas 28
CRAFFIS, Peter 31
CRAFFUS, Nicholas 51
  Peter 51
CRAFLACE, Peter 28
CRAFT, Abraham 68
CRAIG, William 42
CRAVENS, John 70
CRAWFORD, James 34
CREADLEBAUGH, John 64
CRESNER, John 65
CRESSINGER, Orn 65

CRESSWELL, James 46
CRESWELL, Robert 46
CREVENSTON, Nicholas 39
CRICE, Adam 35
CRICHFIELD, William 44
CRIDER, Michael 28
CRIM, Christian 6
CRISMAN, John 1, 35
CRISSMAN William 12
CRISWELL, James 28, 31
  Robert 28
CROHAN, George 38, 39
CROOHAM, James 56
CROSSBEY, James 72
CROSSEN, Thomas 19
CROSSENS, Samuel 48
  Thomas 48
CROSSINGS, Henry 35
CROW, Jacob 55
CROY, Jacob 4, 72
  Richard 3, 72
CROYL, Adam 1
  George 35
  Thomas 1, 35
CRU, David 42
CRUEY Christopher 72
CRYDER, Michael 33, 51, 54
CULBERTSON, John 47
  Robert 5, 13, 35
CUMM, Christopher 44
CUMMING, Robert 23
CUMMINS, Joseph 13
CUNGHAM, James 15
CUNINGHAM, James 17
  Jonathan 3
CUNNINGHAM, George 42
  James 64
CUNTS, John 65
CURLET, John 55
CURPENEY, John 45
CURRY, James 23
  John 23, 48
  William 19, 44

DALTON, James 1, 35
DAMOND, Domnick 56
DANIEL, Edward 12
  John 12
  Samuel 28, 51
DARBY, John 63
DART, John 19, 48
DASON, David 4

DAUGHERTY, Barnard 40, 71
  John 40
DAVID, Eliezer 1
DAVIDSON, Hugh 42
  Samuel 35, 41
DAVIS, ----- 41
  Asiah 56
  Bartholomew 24
  Benjamin 33, 62
  Eleazer 35
  Henry 8, 17, 63, 66
  Isaiah 24
  John 27, 44, 51
  Joshua 16, 63
  Lewis 17, 64
  Nethaniel 64
  Philip 17
  Samuel 33, 53
  Thomas 12, 40, 64
DAVISON, Hugh 24
  Samuel 1
DEAN, James 15, 28, 51
  John 15, 28, 31, 59
  Mathew 54
  Matthew 33
  Samuel 59
  Thomas 15, 59
  William 15, 51, 59
DEBERT, John 1
  Michael 1, 39
DEETS, Yost 9
DELABOUGH, Valentine 60
DELAPT, Richard 1, 4
DELEBAUGH, Valentine 66
DENMER, Isaac 40
DERIMORE, Isaac 12
DERVIE, Henry 13
DEVEE, Henry 69
DEVONBAUGH, Casper 13
DEVONPORT, Josiah 27
DEVOUR, Cornelius 4, 72
  Luke 72
  William 4
DEVOURE, Daniel 72
  William 72
DEWIT, Peter 28, 51
DIBERT, John 35
  Michael 35
DICE, Henry 19
DICK, Widow 28
DICKENS, Thomas 4
DICKENSON, Amos 72
  Thomas 72
DICKEY, James 28, 47
  John 28, 47

INDEX

DICKINSON, Stephen 72
DICKSON, ----- 33
DIDIER, Henry 1
DIGH, Abraham 62
DIMON, Domnic 26
DISHON, Morris 48
DIVER, William 8
DIVINNEY, Andrew 34
DIXON, ----- 54
  William 55
DONACHE, John 24
DONAHE, Joseph 6
DONALD, Andrew 31
DONALDS, Edward 70
DONALDSON, ----- 54
  Andrew 28
  Hugh 63
  Joseph 16, 33
  Moses 59
DONALSON, ----- 71
DONELY, Domneck 40
DONNALD, Dominic 4
DONNELSON, Moses 28
DONOHEW, John 56
DORSEY, Edward 63
DOUGHERTY, Barnard 32, 35
DOVE, William 8
DOWLEN, Michael 15
  Richard 15
DRAKE, Benjamin 28
  George 6
  Jesse 6
  Oliver 6
DRALBAUGH, Valentine 9
DREAK, Benjamin 51
DREENAN, Samuel 35
DRENAN, William 58
DRENNON, Samuel 1
DRUMGOLD, Francis 38
  Thomas 38
DRUPE, Paul 8
DRUSSEL, George 8
DUCKMAN, Ezedekiah 72
DUFFELD, Minister 58
DUGHMAN, Christian 72
  John 72
  Michael 72
DULL, John 44
DUNCAN, Stephen 58
  Steven 27
DUNLAP, James 1, 28, 53
  Richard 74
DUNLOP, James 35
  Jean 35
DUNNING, ----- 38, 39

DUNWOODY, William 6
DURST, Casper 8, 66
DWIRE, Shaphat 11
  Shaphet 66
  William 66

EACHART, Joseph 1
EACHENS, William 28
EACKERT, Frederick 6
EADY, Widow 48
EAGLESON, John 42
EAGO, Frederick 36
EAKEN, William 53
EAKERS, Abia 11
EARLEY, Samuel 58
EARNEST, George 35
  Thomas 70
EARNIST, Adam 1
EARNSBARGER, Powel 44
EASTER, Peter 35, 39
  Valentine 34, 35, 54
EATHENAUR, Joseph 41
EATON, David 53
EBBIT, William 15
ECKLES, William 1, 64
EDDY, Gaven 19
  William 23
EDENTON, Johnathan 42
EDINGTON, David 28
  Jonathan 34
  Philip 34
EDMISTON, Thomas 15
EDMON, Thomas 60
EDMOSTON, John 51
  Thomas 51
EDWARD, Thomas 28
EDWARDS, John 38
  William 24
EGIO, Daniel 52
EGNEW, John 28
EGY, Frederick 1
EKER, Joseph 35
ELBERGER, Jacob 9
ELDER, Arthur 4
  George 15, 40, 59, 71
  John 4, 72
  Joshua 28, 53
ELLINGER, John 1
ELLIOT, ----- 38, 39
  Benjamin 24, 28, 42, 51, 69
  Edward 71
  James 16, 28

  John 24, 27, 69
  Robert 35
  William 4, 36, 39
ELLIOTT, John 58
EMEL, John 48
EMMERT, George 61
  Wentle 31, 60
ENDSLO, Christopher 48
ENGLAND, Henry 41
  James 40
  John 12, 40
ENGLE, Clements 9
ENLOWS, Henry 6
ENOCH, Williams 63
ENSLOW, Christopher 13
  George 13, 19, 69, 70
ENYART, John 14, 59
ERVIN, William 69
ERWIN, ----- 38, 62
  David 36, 63
  Robert 38
ESPY, David 1, 35
ETNIER, John 9
ETNOYER, John 66
ETONER, John 35
EUYART, John 17
EVAN, John 17
EVANS, Edward 4
  Nathan 4
EVENS, Abraham 35
  David 63
  Gerrett 72
  Robert 39
EVERLY, John 6
  Peter 6
EWALT, John 1, 35, 39
EWEN, Alexander 31
  Samuel 31
EWIN, Mr. 68
EWING, Thomas 46
EYART, William 59

FAITH, Abraham 44
  Ruth 6
FALMOTH, Doras 48
FARIS, Thomas 72
FARMER, John 4, 72
  William 12, 40
FAULKENER, Michael 54
FAUTT, Barnard 62
FEATHER, George 1
  Jacob 1
  Michael 33

INDEX

FEATS, George 72
    John 72
    Martin 72
FEE, John 28, 51
FERGUISON, Hugh 69
    John 69
FERGUSON, Henry 28, 46
    Hugh 11
    John 68
    Thomas 29, 46
FETHER, George 36
    Michael 36, 54
FIDLER, Timothy 48
FIKE, Christian 68
    John 9, 66
FIKLE, Daniel 19
FINDLEY, Robert 19
    Samuel 4, 5, 27
FINLAY, Samuel 42, 58, 59, 66, 72, 74
FINNEY, John 38
FIRESTONE, Nicholas 25
FISHER, Jacob 9, 66
    John 19, 48
FITCHPATRICK, John 48
FITSIMMONS, Patrick 25
FITSPATRICK, John 19
FITZIMMONS, Thomas 38
FITZSIMONS, Patrick 42
FLAKE, Henry 9
FLATCHER Archbald 29
    James 1
FLAXENEER, John 47
FLECK, Adam 44
    Henry 66
    Jacob 11, 66
FLEEHARD, James 36
FLEEHARTY, John 12, 40
FLEMING, James 24, 42
FLENIGAN, John 38
FLETCHER, Archibald 51
FLORA, James 15, 59
FOLEY, James 25
FOOLAN, James 59
FORD, John 1, 36
FORDER, William 13
FORKER, Thomas 36
FORREY, Joseph 66
    Peter 66
FOSHEE, Solomon 15
FOSTER, John 16, 59
    Lewis 16
FOUST, Adam 9
    Nicholas 9
FOUTS, Nicholas 66

FOWLEY, James 56
FOX, Frederick 5
    Henry 51
    Jacob 4, 72
    William 30
FRANCIS, John 40
    Williams 30
FRANKLIN, Joseph 25, 56
FRAZER, John 38
    Thomas 4
    William 40
FREDLINE, Lodwick 44
FREDREGIL, William 40
FREDRIGAL, William 13
FREEMAN, John 34
FRENCH, James 70
    Thomas 19
FREY, George 47
    Mr. 68
FRICK, Christian 11
FRIDLINE, Ludwick 6
FRIEND, ----- 35
    Andrew 6, 41
    Charles 6
    John 13, 40
    Joseph 13, 40
FRY, George 28
FUBACK, George 40
FUNK, George 1, 5, 36, 46, 72
FURNEY, Joseph 9
    Peter 9
FURRA, John 9
FURRY, John 66

GABLER, Jacob 9
GAD, Absalom 56
    William 56
GAFF, William 65
GAILBRAITH, John 58
GALAHER, John 74
GALBRAITH, James 25, 56
    Robert 16, 27, 58, 59
GALLAHER, John 25, 43
GALLOHER, ----- 42
GALLOWAY, George 17, 63
    James 18
    John 17, 65
GAMBLE, John 53
GAMEL, John 29
GAMOR, Witho 9
GARDNER, George 36
    Robert 25, 56
GARRY, John 64
GATES, William 23

GATRILL, Francis 15
    John 15
GEORGE, Albright 20
    Joseph 51
    Powel 23
    Powell 23
    William 17, 65
GERARD, Nathaniel 29
GERRET, Nathaniel 51
GETTY, John 66
GIBBINS, Morris 48
GIBBONS, Margarit 12
GIBLER, Jacob 66
GIBLETIN, Philip 48
GIBSON, James 17, 29, 63
    John 12, 69
    Robert 1, 18, 36, 64
    William 12, 14, 17, 65, 70
GIDION, John 49
GILESPY, Samuel 52
GILLAN, Daniel 48
GILLELAN, Philip 20
GILLILAN, William 36
GILMORE, James 6, 11, 44
GILPEN, ----- 33, 54
GINKINS, Benjamin 56
    Even 56
GITTICK, John 9
GLADFIELD, Solomon 9
GLASNER, Henry 9, 66
    Jacob 9, 66
GLASS, John 68
GLENN, Andrew 29, 46
    Archibald 29, 46
    Hugh 25
    John 29, 46
GNAGEY, Christian 66
GODFREY, Nipper 66
GOFFINE, Benjamin 29
GOOD, Jacob 9, 66, 68
GOODEN, Aaron 72
    Moses 72
GOODHART, Andrew 66
GOOSEHORN, George 25
    Jacob 25
    Nicholas 27
GOOSHAIN, Jacob 56
GOOSHORN, George 56
GORDON, David 29, 47
    James 1, 39
    Major 33, 54
    Moses 20, 48
GORMAN, John 34
GRAF, William 17

INDEX

GRAFF, George 11
  Peter 9
GRAHAM, Edward 17, 23, 63
  John 1, 36
  Moses 20, 23
  Widow 20, 48
GRAHAMS, John 20
  William 20
GRANT, Yoast 36
GRATH, John 12
GRAVE, Peter 66
GRAVES, Samuel 20, 48
GRAY, Absolam 34
  Aramanus 34
  George 46
  Robert 23
  Thomas 46
GREATHOUSE, William 6
GREEN, Andrew 38
  Joseph 25, 56
  Thomas 6
GREGG, ----- 39
  John 36
GRIFFITH, David 11, 66
  Ebenezer 11
  John 11, 68
GRIFITH, Ebenezer 66
GRIGG, John 1
GRIM, Hugh 56
  Jacob 56
GRIPE, Daniel 33
  Jacob 33
GRIPES, Jacob 54
GRISSING, Arnd 9
GRONER, John 9, 66
GROSE, George 60
GULLIFORD, John 33
  Widow 33, 53
  William 34
GUNDY, Joseph 66
  Mathias 66
GUTHERY, Daniel 59
  Hugh 59
GUTHRIE, Daniel 14
  Hugh 16
  John 20

HACLER, Martin 48
HADE, William 25
HAGAN, John 13
HAGGAN, John 40
HAIN, Nicholas 40
HAINES, John 72
HAINS, Ruben 47
  Thomas 42

HAIR, Christian 66
HAKERSMITH, Jacob 48
HALL, Jacob 29, 51
  Samuel 13, 40
  Thomas 11, 40
HAMBLER, Andrew 48
HAMBOUGH, George 9
HAMET, Edward 6
HAMIL, Robert 18
HAMILL, Nethaniel 64
HAMILTON, John 18, 41
  Robert 64
  Thomas 12, 40
HAMMEL, John 18
  Nathaniel 18
HAMMILL, John 64
  Robert 64
HAMPSON, James 15, 59
HANCE, Morrison 29
  Wentle 16
HANES, Abraham 29
  Daniel 5
  Reuben 16, 33
HANNABLE, William 44
HANNAH, James 56
HANOWALT, Henry 16
HARDEN, Ignatius 14
  Thomas 4
HARDESTER, Henry 56
HARDISTY, Richard 4
HARLIN, Jacob 39
HARMINTAGE, Jacob 29
HARR, Christian 9
HARRIS, John 27, 47
HARSH, Jacob 1
HARSHBERGER, John 9
HART, William 20, 48
HARTFORD, Patrick 1, 36
HARTLEN, Leonard 5
HARTSEL, Jacob 6
HARVEY, James 38
  John 56
  Josiah 62
HASSON, Jacob 11
HAVERSACK, Henry 20
HAWKINS, George 48
  George Frazer 23
HAY, Simon 9, 66
  Thomas 2
  Valentine 9
HAYS, Thomas 36
HEAD, Edward 18, 63
  Peter 23
  William 23, 43
HEANEY, Patrick 40

HEANS, Abraham 51
  Ruben 42
HEANY, Patrick 13
HEATER, George 16, 59
HELM, Dinnis 36
  Frederick 36
  Jacob 36
  John 36
HEMPHILL, Adley 1, 36
HENDERSHALD, Balser 48
HENDERSHET, Jacob 48
HENDERSHOT, Jacob 20
HENDERSON, Harvey 58
  James 66
HENDRICKS, James 11
  John 9
HENDRIX, James 66
  John 66
HENMAN, Philip 66
HENRY, Elizabeth 36
  James 2, 38
  Peter 48
  Robert 59
  William 2, 27, 33, 39, 54, 59
HER, Jacob 36
  Laurence 36
HERMAN, Charles 6
HEROD, John 18
  Thomas 65
HESS, Henry 61
  William 48
HESSE, John 34
HEY, Felty 66
HIEPETER, George 4
HIET, John 6
HIGGINS, Edward 32
HILL, Frederick 13, 40
  George 20, 48
  Hugh 15
  John 48
  Nethaniel 56
HINEBOCH, George 66
  John 66
HINES, Henry 13, 59
  John 4
  Joseph 4
HINESH, Henry 16
HINISH, Henry 70
HITE, John 2
HITER, John 66
HOBORN, Joseph 29
HOCKERSMITH, Conred 23
HODGE, Thomas 25, 56

INDEX

HOFMAN, George 60
  Jacob 60
HOFSTOTLER, Christian 9
HOGAR, Philip 72
HOGLAND, Tobias 72
HOLIDAY, Adam 53
  James 33
  Samuel 53
  Thomas 29
  William 34, 36, 54, 56
HOLLARD, Henry 69
  Mathias 69
HOLLE, John 44
HOLLER, Henry 14
  Matthias 12
HOLLEY, David 60
HOLLIDAY, William 25, 53, 54
HOLLINSHEAD, James 48
HOLT, Henry 25, 43
HOLTZ, Jacob 12, 40
HOOD, John 68
HOOP, George 20, 48
HOOPER, ----- 32, 45
  Robert Latis 62
HOOPINGARNER, George 49
HOOT, John 9
HOOVER, Adam 9, 45
  Casper 9, 66
  Henry 18, 63
  Jacob 18
  John 18, 63, 66
HORSE, George 48
HORT, John 36
HOSER, John 54
HOSHEL, Henry 34
HOSS, John George 20
HOSTALER, Christian 66
  John 66
HOSTELLER, Jacob 66
HOUGH, Jacob 20, 48
HOUSER, Christian 36
  John 34
HOVER, Adam 66
  John 9
HOWDERSHELT, Christopher 23
HOY, Daniel 32
  David 2
HOYL, Walter 9
HOYLE, Walter 66
HOYSTOTLER, Jacob 9
HUBBS, Thomas 41
HUBLEY, Adam 62
HUCK, George 45

HUDSON, Andrew 72
  George 25, 43
HUFF, Elisha 40
HUFFMAN, Jacob 31
HUFFNAGLE, Michael 42, 60
HUFFNAWGLE, Michael 34
HUGGUN, George 31
HUGHES, Samuel 42
HULEN, Elisabeth 6
  Isaac 6
HULL, Elisabeth 32
  Solomon 20
HULLY, David 32
HUMBERT, Friderick 18
HUMBURD, Frederick 63
HUNT, William 20, 48
HUNTER, ----- 27
  Alexander 66
  Charles 45
  David 63
  George 45, 62
  James 33, 58, 71
  John 18, 62
  Samuel 16
  Thomas 25, 58
  William 18, 43, 65
HUNTSMAN, John 11
HUSBANDS, Harman 6
  Herman 32, 44
HUSKINS, William 61
HUSTEN, Andrew 4
  William 43
HUSTON, Alexander 4, 72
  Edward 5, 72
  Robert 5, 72
  William 46
HUTCHESON, George 47
  William 43
HUTCHISON, George 29
  William 27
HYDER, John 9
HYNS, Henry 44
HYSOP, Samuel 29, 52
HYSTOTLER, John 9

IEMS, John 72
IGO, Daniel 28
IGOE, James 34
  Joshua 34
ILER, Honacle 2
  Jacob 2
  Nicholas 36
IMLER, George 2, 36
INGLE, Clemens 66

INNINGS, Benjamin 6
IRWIN, David 1, 17
  Joseph 32
  William 12
IZER, Philip 64

JACK, ----- 58
JACKSON, George 29, 52
  Thomas 18, 64
JACOBS, Daniel 63
JAMES, William 40
JAQUES, Thomas 64
JARVIS, Henry 34
JEFERES, Jesse 56
JENKINS, Evan 20
  John 15
JEWEL, George 62
JILES, ----- 28, 47
JINKINS, Benjamin 62
  Even 56
  Ewen 49
  John 59
JOHN, David 63
  Jacob 18, 63
  James 63
  John 18
  Thomas 18, 64
JOHNS, Robert 25
JOHNSON, Anthony 52
  James 52
  John 56
  Lawyer 53
  Thomas 52
  William 46, 53
JOHNSTON, ----- 59
  James 25, 29, 34
  John 2, 36
  Joseph 12, 15, 17, 40
  Robert 25, 43
  Samuel 29
  Thomas 12, 29, 31, 40
  William 29
JOLLEY, Benjamin 32
JONES, ----- 23, 54
  Amos 13, 70
  Andrew 11, 70
  David 6, 45
  Ezekiel 6
  Isaac 45
  John 6
  Joseph 9, 67
  Robert 6, 45
  William 40, 45

INDEX

JOULER, Jacob 9
JOYL, Nelson 20
JUDY, Matthias 11
JUSTICE, James 64
    William 25

KAIN, Moses 51
KAIR, Robert 49
KAM, Charles 15
KARR, William 53
KASEBEAR, John 2
KEER, Acquilla 26
KEETH, ----- 59
    Adam 59
KEEVER, Jacob 32
    Martin 6
    Michael 6
    Peter 9
KEFFER, Adam 6
    Jacob 9, 61
    Michael 9
KEGG, Nicholas 12, 40
KEGLER, Jacob 48
KEITH, Adam 15
    Michael 15
KELLEY, John 27
KELLY, John 44
    Joseph 4, 72
    Mathew 4, 72
    Matthias 13
    William 25
KELSEY, Robert 27
KENARD, John 49
KENDALL, John 63
    Robert 65
KENDEL, John 18
    Robert 18
KENEDY, David 42
KENNEDY, David 29, 31,
    47, 52
    Francis 52
    James 29, 52
    John 29
    Simon 43
    William 36
KENTON, John 2, 38
    Rachel 2, 36
    Thomas 2, 36
KERNAHEN, Michael 15
KERR, Acquilla 27
    John 56
    Robert 20
    Samuel 18, 64
KERSMAN, Martin 69
KEY, John 15

KIDD, Benjamin 16, 23,
    49, 59
KIGER, Anthony 16
KIMBER, James 29
    Richard 14, 70
KIMBERLIN, John 6
KIMBLE, ----- 61
    George 31, 61
    Michael 61
    Peter 20
    Petter 49
    Philip 6, 32, 61
KIMEL, Jacob 45
KING, Christian 9, 67
    George 56
    John 67
    Michael 45
    Richard 15
KIRKPATRICK, John 6
    Moses 25
KISBEER, William 44
KIZAR, Christian 58
KLINK, John 9
KNAVE, Jacob 34
KNEGEY, Christian 9
KNIPPER, Godfrey 9
KOOCK, Adam 9
KOWELL, Christian 20
KUZER, Adam 72

LAFALY, Adam 67
LAFFERTY, John 2, 36
LAIN, Wilkinson 56
LAINE, Henry 72
LAISHER, John 4
    Thomas 4
LAMAN, Benedict 67
    Jacob 49
    John 67
LAMB, Laurince 4
    Timothy 4
    Widow 20
LAMBE, John 73
    Lawrence 72
    Timothy 73
LAMBERD, George 49
LAMBERT, George 20, 62
    Jacob 61
    Thomas 62
LAMISTER, Richard 4
LANCASTER, John 20
LANCE, Christian 20
    Christopher 49
LANCEL, George 39

LANE, Corban 25
    Dutton 25
    Samuel 25
    Wilkison 25
LAPLE, Peter 67
LATAN, William 49
LATON, Asher 49
    Obadiah 49
    Samuel 49
LATTA, John 25, 56
LAWSON, Anthony 18
LAYMAN, Peter 11
LAZER, John 72
    Joseph 72
    Thomas 72
LEAK, Nicholas 49
LEAMEN, Benedick 9
LEAN, Daniel 56
    Samuel 56
    William 15
LEARD, Jacob 52
LEATON, Asher 20
    Obadia 20
    Samuel 20
    William 20
LEBARGER, George 72
    Ludwick 72
LEBARIGAR, Nicholas 72
LEE, Francis 18
LEECH, Henry 36
    Nicholas 20
    Steven 20
LEEP, Peter 9
LEINHART, Enoch 7
    George 7
LEMAN, Benedict 67
LEMON, George 61
    Peter 61
    Thomas 18
LENNON, Patrick 46
LEONARD, Patrick 29
LEVI, Levi Andrew 2, 39
LEWIS, Elizabeth 29
    John 31
    Joshua 29
    Ruth 16
    Thomas 64
LIBERGAR, Ludwick 4
LIBERGER, Nicoles 4
LICKEN, ----- 50
LIDDY, Joseph 72
LIGHTMAN, Georg 40
LILLEY, Richard 15, 60

INDEX

LINN, Adam 18, 62
  Adis 20
  Isaac 20, 49
  James 56
  John 64
  Levi 20
  Widow 20, 49
  William 65
LINSEY, Samuel 33
  William 38
LIPPS, Philip 23
LITLE, Captain 54
  John 46, 60
LITTLE, Captain 33
  James 29
  John 16, 29
LIVERGOOD, Peter 67
LIVINGOOD, Peter 9
LIVINGSTON, Henry 11, 69
  John 13, 69
LLOYD, David 31
  Henry 29
LOAN, Benjamin 2, 36
LOAR, George 61
LOARE, John 45
LOCK, Thomas 56
LOGAN, Hugh 56
  James 56
  William 56
LOGUE, Hugh 46
LONG, ----- 55
  Benjamin 25, 27, 56
  Hugh 46
  John 25
  Joseph 29, 46
  Thomas 31, 46
  William 25, 29, 56
LONGSTRETH, Bartholomew 20
  James 49
  John 20, 49
  Martin 20, 49
  Philip 20, 49
LOUT, Daniel 7
  Jacob 7, 45
  Valentine 9
LOVE, James 27, 56
  John 56
  Robert 12, 40
LOVEALL, Jonathan 25, 43
LOW, Richard 72
  Ritchard 4
LOWDER, Widow 20
LOWER, George 32

LOWREY, Abraham 18
  Alexander 33, 54, 65
  David 34, 54
LOYD, Henry 52
LUCAS, George 43
LUFFBORROUGH, John 6
  Jonathan 6
LUIES, John 56
LUKENS, ----- 27
LUSK, Robert 5, 73
LYND, James 25
LYON, William 33, 54

M, Daniel 63
MACAUNE, John 49
MACLANE, Jacob 49
  James 49
MADDEN, John 63
MAGAW, ----- 58
  David 53
MAGHAN, Thomas 40
MAGINES, Charles 57
MAGLAHALAN, William 56
MAKY, Nicholas 2
MALOT, Benjamin 49
  John 49
  Obadiah 49
  Theadras 49
MAN, Andrew 21, 49
MARDIS, John 65
MARIS, Mathias 46, 68
MARKER, George 10
  Henry 10, 67
  Mathias 67
MARKLEY, Jacob 11, 68
  John 10, 67
MARLEY, ----- 33
MARSHAL, James 43
MARTEN, John 49
MARTIN, Edward 49
  Hugh 63
  Jacob 63
  James 69
  John 18, 34, 64
  Thomas 23
  William 14
MARTON, John 49
  Richard 49
  William 49
MASE, James 38
MASON, Jacob 49
  John 20, 25, 57
  Philip 10, 67
  William 25, 57
MASSOON, John 49

MAST, Christian 67
MASTERS, William 73
MATHER, Joseph 62
MATHES, George 67
MATHIAS, Philip 43, 67
  Thomas 59
MATTHEWS, Thomas 27
MATTHIAS, George 9
  Philip 10
MAUGH, Jacob 36
MAXWELL, James 18
  Patrick 18
MAY, George 70
  John Andrew 1
MAYANDREW, John 36
McALEAS, Menasah 57
McALEVEY, William 46
McANARY, Susanna 7
McANEAR, Andrew 62
McARDEL, James 25
McAULEY, Cornelius 2
McBRIDE, James 25, 43
McCALL, William 2
McCAMON, Samuel 57
McCANNA, Hugh 15
McCARDY, James 15
McCARTNEY, Robert 46
McCASHLEN, Samuel 36
McCASHLIN, Samuel 2
McCAULEY, Cornelius 36
McCLEAN, Allen 15
  George 21
  Jacob 23
  James 23
McCLEES, Manassah 25
McCLELAN, James 64
  John 18, 53, 64
  Royer 26
McCLELLAND, John 18
McCLEMENS, John 13
McCLEWN, James 43
McCOMBS Allen 36
McCONNEL, Alexander 18
  Daniel 18
  William 58
McCONNELL, Alexander 62
  Daniel 63
  James 64
McCORD, James 43
McCORDY, Daniel 63
McCORMICK, Alexander 29, 46
  James 18, 21
  John 14

INDEX

McCREA, John 25
  Thomas 64
McCUNE, Thomas 53
McCURDY, Daniel 18
McDANIEL, Thomas 12
  William 12, 41
McDERMOTT, Edward 46
  James 46
McDONALD, Duncan 43
  James 60
  Joseph 70
  Rowland 42
  Widow 70
  William 69
McDOWEL, Nathan 43
McDOWELL, James 64
  Nathan 25
  William 25, 43
McELROY, Alexander 25, 43
McELVEAN, William 52
McELVY, William 29
McENTIRE, Daniel 7
McFALL, Widow 18
McFARREN, Joseph 70
McFEETERS, James 56
McFERREN, Joseph 13
McGAUGHEY, Arthur 36
  John 36
  Thomas 38
McGAUGHY, Arthur 2
McGAVOCK, Benjamin 46
McGAW, ----- 27, 60
  David 29
  Robert 15, 27
McGEE, Thomas 23
McGILL, Jean 25
McGINNES, Charles 25
  James 29, 51
McGRAW, Edward 15
McGUIRE, Bartely 51
  Bartholomew 29
  John 34
  Patrick 34
McKARTY, Daniel 69
McKEE, Alexander 38
  James 21, 25, 43
McKEEVER, John 12
McKENNEY, James 49
  Joseph 49
  Robert 49
McKEVER, John 40
McKINLAY, John 63
  Joseph 63
McKINLEY, John 18

McKINNEY, John 21, 70
  Joseph 21
  Robert 21
McKRACHEN, James 57
McLAIMANS, Samuel 57
McLAIN, John 64
McLAMINS, John 70
McLELAN, James 67
McMATH, Samuel 24, 57
McMICHAEL, Daniel 41
  John 38
  Mary 45
McMOULTRIE, David 25, 29
McMOULTRY, David 59
McMOUTRY, David 52
McMULLEN, Alexander 32
  James 2, 36
  Thomas 32
McMUTREY, David 46
McNEEL, Hector 36
McNIGHT, Patrick 7
McPHETRO, James 25
McSPARRAN, Duncan 36
McSPARREN, Duncan 21
McUNE, John 21
MEAD, George 38
MEANS, ----- 29
  Daniel 12, 69
  Hugh 14, 29, 33, 42, 53, 54
MEASE, James 38
MEGIBENS, Thomas 70
MELICK, John 67
MELOT, Theodorus 20
MELOTT, John 20, 21
  Obadiah 21
MENDAIR, Alexander 45
MERCHANT, ----- 59
MERDAC, James 25
MERIS, Matthias 7
MICHAEL, Andrew 25, 56
  Daniel 40
  Henry 73
  Paul 73
MICKEY, Daniel 68
MIFFLIN, ----- 29
MIFLEN, Samuel 47
MIFLIN, Samuel 53
MILBORN, John 49
MILEY, Abraham 13, 40, 41
MILLEGAN, George 2
MILLEN, Edman 2

MILLER, Abraham 61
  Adam 13, 70
  Christian 10, 67
  Christopher 32, 61
  Edmund 39
  Felix 14
  George 11, 49
  Henry 55
  Isaac 31, 61
  Jacob 2, 7, 14, 36, 45, 70
  James 25
  John 10, 32, 45, 61, 67
  Joseph 34
  Margaret 36
  Michael 10, 67
  Nicholas 10
  Peter 67
  Phillip 49
  Richard 46
  Thomas 14, 17
  William 11, 67
MILLHOUSE, Jacob 10
MILLIGAN, George 36, 39
MILLOR, John 2
MINER, John 53
MIRES, Mathias 14, 32
  Matthias 11
  Peter 11
MISHLER, Joseph 67
MITCHEL, James 7
  John 7, 29, 52
  Robert 52
MITCHELL, Mr. 60
MOBLEY, Ezekiel 16
MOLTON, John 60
MONEY, Barnard 49
  Barnet 20
  Jacob 21
MONTGOMERY, John 2, 21, 57
  Samuel 51
  Thomas 51
MOORE, Andrew 41
  Daniel 34, 54
  Frances James 7
  James 41
  John 11, 25, 43, 57, 69
  Levi 14, 60
  Robert 11, 40, 41, 70
  Samuel 11, 69
  William 34, 54
  Zebulon 60
  Zebulun 15

INDEX

MOOREHEAD, Thomas 34
MORAN, Edward 4
  George 21
MOREHEAD, John 70
MOREHOUSE, Widow 20
MORGAN, ----- 38, 47, 53
  John 25, 57
  Peter 45
  Phelix 7
  Thomas 26
  William 15
MORNINGSTAR, Daniel 7, 46
  Jacob 7, 44
MORRIS, John 4
  Joseph 62
  Robert 54, 74
  William 25, 57
MORRISAN, Joseph 4
MORRISON, Benjamin 23
  John 58
  Joseph 11, 69
MORROW, Thomas 57
  Widow 57
MORSE, Samuel 40
MORTIMER, James 70
  John 34, 69
MORTON, Edward 20
  James 25, 43
  John 16, 20, 29, 44, 52
  Richard 20
  Samuel 27
  Thomas 20
  William 20
MOSS, Samuel 12
MOSSER, John 45
MOSSTALLER, Frederick 10
MOST, Jacob 67
MOSTALLER, Frederick 32
MOSTOLLER, Frederick 67
MOTE, Jacob 10
MOUNTAIN, Joseph 7
MOWNEY, John 49
MULHOLAM, Hugh 43
MULLEN, James 15
MURPHY, Alexander 12, 40
  Henderson 11
  Thomas 25, 57
MURREY, Hugh 57
MURRY, James 11, 49, 63
MUSTLER, Joseph 9
MYARS, George 63
  Mathias 70
MYERS, Daniel 18
  Frederick 63
  Jacob 29

NAGLE, Frederick 36
NAWGLE, ----- 3
  Anthony 2, 37
  Barnard 10
  Frederick 10, 68
NEARHOFF, John 52
NEASBET, Jean 64
NEEMIRE, Jacob 73
  John 73
  Peter 73
  William 2, 37
NEEMYAR, Isaac 4
NEHEMIAH, Michael 21
NELSON, Abraham 30
  William 30
NEMIER, John 5
NERON, Joseph 34
NESBIT, Widow 18
NICE, Cristman 73
NICHOLESON, Hugh 45
NICHOLSON, Hugh 7
  William 7
NILSON, Abraham 46
  Robert 46
  William 46
NIXON, George 2, 37, 71
  Robert 27
NOBLE, David 10
  Henry 7
  James 45
NORTON, Thomas 70

O'NEAL, Peter 14
O'REILLY, Peter 34
OAKS, John 16, 64
OBURN, Joseph 46
OGDEN, Joseph 62
OGLAND, Daniel 23
OHARA, Arthur 40
OLEY, Shrock 67
OLINGER, John 43, 67
OLLINGER, John 10
ONEAL, Peter 70
ONGAR, Henry 21
ONGER, George 23
ORBISON, ----- 33, 54
ORGAN, David 37
ORLTON, Hugh 26, 43
ORMSBY, John 71
OTT, Wendle 65
  Wentel 18
OUGHWICK, ----- 58
OWENS, Widow 18

PALM, Adam 10
PANNEL, Thomas 12
PANTHER, Godfrey 34
PARE, Ludwick 67
PARISH, Joseph 57
PARKER, John 73
PARKS, William 47
PARONE, Nicholas 7
PARR, ----- 33, 53
  Elihu 7
  Sarah 45
PARRON, John 40
PATERSON, James 40
  William 47
PATH, ----- 39
PATTEN, Matthew 26
PATTERSON, James 13, 30
  Joseph 30
  William 18, 30, 57, 65
PATTON, ----- 42
  John 52
  Mathew 57
PAUL, John 62
  William 57
PAXTEN, Thomas 18
PAXTON, John 18, 69
  Samuel 4, 73
  Thomas 64
PECK, Benjamin 62
  George 11, 21, 49
  John 49, 70
PEETERS, John 32
  Richard 74
PEMBERTON, Israel 54
PENN, Jonathan 21
PENNAL, Thomas 69
PENROD, David 61
  John 7, 32, 45, 61
  Peter 61
  Solomon 32, 61
  Tobias 45
PERKEY, Abraham 67
  Jacob 67
  Peter 67
PERKLEY, Ludwick 67
PERKY, Christian 67
PERREY, ----- 58
PERRY, ----- 27
  Samuel 2, 5, 58, 60, 74
PERSONS, John 57
PETERS, John 2
  Richard 5, 33, 54, 74
PHAGAN, Joseph 14
PHILIP, Francis 45

INDEX

PHILIPS, Cathrine 62
  Evan 18
  William 16, 34
PHISICK, Edmond 39
PICKET, Heathcock 57
  Hethcott 26
PILE, Casper 7, 45
PIPER, John 13, 70
  Luesanda 16
PITMAN, Joseph 21
  Richard 21, 49
  William 21, 49
PITTMAN, Richard 21, 64
PLATER, Joseph 23
PLEASANT, Samuel 33, 45, 54
PLOWCH, Elizabeth 67
PLUMMER, Abraham 16, 17
  Isaac 4, 73
  John 14
PLUNKET, Doctor 39
  Robert 7
POLARD, William 57
POLLARD, William 26
POLLOCK, James 62
  John 26, 39, 43
POLLOM, Adam 67
POORMAN, Jacob 49, 63
PORTER, James 46
  John 2, 39
  Samuel 30
  William 30, 46
PORTON, John 73
POTTESON, Thomas 49
POTTS, Jonathan 73
POWEL, George 48
  John 49
  Joseph 49
POWELL, Joseph 21
PRETER, Thomas 33
PRICE, Merriman 57
PRIDEBAKER, Abraham 7
PRIGMORE, Jonathan 52
  Joseph 30, 52
  Theodoras 60
PROCTOR, Thomas 62
  William 2, 37
PROSER, Daniel 73
PUMPUAH, Conred 34
PURDUE, William 5, 73
PURSEL, Benjamin 7
  James 7
  John 7
PURVINES, ----- 42
PUTTEN, Charles 7

QUERY, John 18
QUIGLEY, John 58
QUIN, Patrick 21

RALPH, David 16
RALSTON, David 30, 46
RAMSEY, James 63
  John 26, 43
  Robert 26, 43
  William 26, 43
RANALDS, George 52
RANKEN, John 63
RANKIN, James 63
  John 18
RAVER, Christopher 50
READ, John 7
REAGH, John 57
REAMON, Godfrey 61
REED, John 30, 32, 53
  Joseph 46
  Moses 21, 49
  William 60
REESE, Detrict 62
REETER, Peter 32
REEVES, Abner 21
  John 14
  Thomas 11
REGAN, Fergus 40
REINHART, David 2
REYNOLD, Francis 21
REYNOLDS, Francis 13, 14, 70
  George 30
  James 59
  John 21
RHEA, Thomas 4, 73
RHOADS, Daniel 4
  Gabriel 2, 37
  Henry 7, 45
  Jacob 4, 31, 73
  John 7, 31, 45, 61
  Joseph 4, 31, 73
RICE, Frederick 73
  Jacob 73
RICHARD, Frederick 2
RICHEY, Gideon 13
  John 13, 69
RICKETS, Cheany 30
  Cheney 46, 51
  Edward 52, 60
  Ezekiah 52
  Jeremiah 30, 46
RIDDLE, David 30
  Robert 30, 46
RIDEHART, Daniel 62

RIDGES, James 12
RIELEY, Martin 37
  Peter 57
RIENHART, John 40
RIGHART, Frederick 37
RIGHT, David 32
RIGS, James 40
RIND, Joseph 18
RINE, Jacob 2
RINGER, Adam 11, 67
RIPLEOGL, Rinhart 40
RIPPLE, Jacob 7
RIPPLEOGLE, Reinhart 13
RISE, George 45
ROBERTS, Abner 50
  William 7, 62
ROBERTSON, Hugh 61
  Jeremiah 43
  William 62
ROBISON, Abraham 34
  Hugh 10, 67
ROBONY, Nathaniel 21
RODDY, Alexander 30, 47
  James 33, 53
ROIER, Jacob 45
ROISE, Frederick 4
ROLIN, Jacob 40
ROLLER, Jacob 34, 52
ROMACH, George 37
ROMICK, George 2
ROSE, Allen 2, 37
  Cutliph 7
  Edward 13, 40
  James 38
  Jeremiah 57
  Lewis 7
  William 2, 37
ROSS, Doctor 5
  James 61
ROUGH, George 67
ROWLAND, Keenan 70
ROYCE, Aaron 7
  Elisabeth 7
  George 7
  John 7
ROYER, Daniel 18, 63
RUBY, Charles 2, 37
RUFE, Matthias 14
  Michael 12
  Nicholas 13
RUFF, Mathias 40
  Michael 40
  Nicholas 40
  Peter 40
RULON, Nathanel 50

INDEX

RUSH, David 21
  Harry 50
  Henery 50
  Henry 21
  Jacob 21, 23, 50
  John 21, 23, 50
  Peter 21, 23, 50
  Widow 21
  William 7
RUSHE, John 30
RUSHEE, Thomas 47
RUSSELL, John 14
  William 13
RUTLEDGE, Jason 14
RUTTER, Alexander 26, 57
  George 62
  Henry 62
  John 57
  William 57
RYAN, Timothy 37
RYEN, Timothy 2

SALMON, William 19
SAMPLE, David 74
SAMPSON, Hugh 37
  Samuel 13
  William 14
SAMSON, Samuel 22
SAMUEL, Adam 2, 3, 37
  Conred 3
  Conrod 37
SANDERS, Benjamin 15
SAP, Frederick 68
SATORIOUS, William 3
SATORIUS, William 37
SAUNDERS, ----- 60
SAVER, Frederick 10
SAYLOR, Jacob 2, 37, 41
  John 10
SCHREECHFIELD, Benjamin 73
  John 73
SCOTT, James 74
  John 63
  Margaret 64
  Robert 18, 64, 65
  Widow 53
SCOVEL, William 3
SCOVIL, William 37
SCREECHFIELD, Nathaniel 4, 73
SEABROOKS, William 34
SEALLY, Cornelius 12
SEAMANS, Cornelius 70
SECKMAN, John 45

SEDEN, John 57
SEES, George 31
SEEVER, Frederick 4
SELLARS, Joseph 54
SELLER, Andrew 50
SELLERS, Joseph 34
SELLY, Charles 22
SEMPLETON, John 73
SENSENIG, John 45
SERVER, Phelty 3
SEVER, Frederick 73
SHACKLER, Frederick 16
SHACKLEY, George 68
SHADE, ----- 58
SHALLUS, Boston 10
  Conrad 10
  Jacob 16
SHANNON, George 37
SHARAH, Jacob 26
  John 26
SHARAW, John 57
SHAROW, Isaac 57
  Jacob 57
SHAUB, Sebastian 16
SHAULES, Coonrod 67
SHAULS, Boston 67
SHAVER, George 7, 10, 68
  Jacob 7
  John 12, 15, 30, 52, 60, 69, 70
  Mathias 22
  Nicholas 70
  Simon 32
  Tise 50
SHEA, John 30, 47
SHEATS, Henry 14
SHECK, George 61
SHECKLEY, George 60
  Peter 73
SHECKLIN, William 57
SHEE, Francis 63
SHEETS, Delman 10
  Henry 60
  Ludwick 68
  Mathias 4, 73
  Solomon 68
SHEFER, John 22
SHEFFER, George 61
  Henry 61
  Jacob 45
  Philip 61
  Simon 61
SHEILDS, James 43
SHELAR, Harman 50

SHELBY, Evan 19
  Even 63
SHENFELT, George 67
SHENIFELT, George 10
  John 10
SHERER, Andrew 73
SHERLEY, Richard 15
  William 15, 60
SHERTS, George 63
SHIELDS, James 26
  Thomas 30
SHINGLEDECKER, George 23
SHINGLESPARRIGER, Ulric 31
SHINGLETAKER, Jacob 22, 50
  Michael 23
SHINTELTAKER, George 50
SHIPEN, Joseph 47
SHIPPEN, Edward 54
  Joseph 54
SHIPPEY, Edward 33
  Joseph 33
SHIRLEY, ----- 59
SHOCK, George 14
  Jacob 50
SHOEMAKER, George 38
SHOFFE, John 45
SHOLTZ, Nicholas 67
SHOPE, Jacob 60
  John 7
  Sebastine 60
SHRACK, Casper 10
SHROCK, Jacob 10
SHUGAR, ----- 59
SHULL, Adam 19
SHULLER, Harmer 22
SHUTES, Nicholas 10
SHUTTER, Martin 32
SHWARTS, Matthew 12
SIBAL, John 64
SIGLER, John 61
SILL, ----- 39
SILLER, Jacob 67
  John 67
SILLS, Abraham 15, 52
  Anthony 30, 52
  George 3, 37
  Lodwick 52
  Ludwick 30
  Michael 3, 31, 37, 61
  Solomon 14, 52, 60
SILVERSON, Thomas 5

INDEX

SIMMERMAN, Henry 50
  John 22
  Yost 67
SIMMONS, Cornelius 12
SIMONTON, William 34, 54
SIMPSON, Hue 2
  James 64
  James Liddle 19
  Luke 2, 37
SIPES, Charles 22
  Henry 22
  Peter 68
  Thomas 6
SIPS, Charles 50
  Hennery 50
SKEDMORE, Joshua 47
SKELLEY, Hugh 14
  Michal 14
SKIDMORE, Joshua 30
SKILES, Ephraim 60
SKINGLEBARGE, Albright 61
SKINNER, Nathaniel 7
  Reuben 7
  Samuel 2, 7, 37
SLAUGHTER, John 50
  Widow 21
SLEE, Francis 18
SLIDEY, Joseph 4
SLIKER, Laurince 21
SLOAN, William 65
SMALLMAN, Thomas 60
SMART, William 16, 60
SMITH, Adam 21, 50
  Anthony 42
  Casper 26, 57
  Daniel 3, 37
  David 69
  Doctor 39, 74
  Emanuel 22, 50
  Ezekiel 22, 30, 53
  George 3, 38
  Henry 22
  Jacob 34, 61, 68
  James 30, 32, 47, 70
  John 19, 22, 31, 50, 61, 70
  Joseph 68
  Peter 3, 21, 37, 50, 59, 71
  Philip 10, 67
  Rebekah 37
  Robert 30, 47
  Thomas 1, 2, 11, 53, 69,
  Widow 43

  William 27, 30, 33, 38, 42, 53, 54
  Zachariah 50
SMOKER, Jacob 61
SMOOKER, Jacob 32
SNIDER, Adam 22
  Coonrod 43
  Henry 22, 50
  Jacob 10, 68
  Ralph 74
SOCK, Jacob 22
SOOCH, Yost 67
SOOCK, Jacob 68
SOOTER, Martin 61, 67
SOURLEY, Henry 23
SOUSLEY, Henry 21
SOUTH, Francis 12, 69
SOWLER, Henery 50
SPADE, John 57
SPARKS, Joseph 12, 69
SPEAR, Edward 63
SPENCER, James 7, 34
  John 52
  Robert 31
SPIGAR, Christian 10
SPIKER, Christopher 61
  Samuel 10, 61
SPRENDIRON, Michael 68
SPRINGER, Philip 31, 61
SPURGEN, Ezekil 41
  James 41
  John 73
  Samuel 41
SPURGEON, Ezekiel 12
  John 4
  Samuel 12
SQUIRES, George 73
SROCK, Casper 68
STACKMAN, John 69
STAFFORD, Thomas 22, 50
STALL, Hennery 50
  Michael 21
STAM, Alexander 21, 23
  John 10
  Leonard 11
STAMM, Alexander 11
STANDIFORD, Benjamin 26, 57
STANELY, John 50
STANES, George 26
  William 27
STANLEY, Elisabeth 23
  John 22
STANSBEY, Nathan 4
STARK, Philip 15

STAUB, Frederick 50
STEEL, Andrew 3, 37, 74
  John 27
STELL, Edward 62
STEPHENS, Amos 62
  Benjamin 62
  Giles 57
  Richard 64
  Thomas 43, 64
  William 44
STEVEN, Richard 19
STEVENS, Abednego 22
  Abednigo 50
  Benjamin 19, 57
  Giles 26
  John 34, 54
  Richard 22, 50
  Sarah 57
  Thomas 26
  William 22, 50
  Zachariah 26
STEVENSON, John 57
  Robert 47
STEVINS, Amos 18
  John 33
  Thomas 18
STEWART, Alexander 33
  David 34
  James 12, 18
  Samuel 57
STICKLET, Peter 3
STIFFLER, Peter 3
STIFLER, Peter 37
STIKER, Lawrence 50
STILES, David 26, 43
STILLWELL, Elias 22, 50
  Jeremiah 22
  John 22
  Truax 64
STITT, John 26, 43
  Thomas 44
STITTS, Frederick 21
STOMM, John 67
  Leonard 67
STONER, Christian 68
  Christopher 10
  Philip 16, 34, 60
STONG, Adam 57
STORM, Daniel 7
  Henry 14
STOTLER, Casper 31, 61
  Martin 14
STOTSMAN, Jacob 67
STOVER, Christofer 22
STOY, Daniel 61
STRAHON, Thomas 7

89

INDEX

STRAIGHT, William 50
STRAWBRIDGE, Robert 26
STRONG, Philip 60
STUART, Alexander 54
  Andrew 59
  David 54
STUMP, John 10, 69
SUCK, Abraham 43
SULIVAN, Henry 52
  Patrick 45
SULLIVAN, Henry 31
  Patrick 27
SUMMERVAIL, James 37, 57
SUTTER, Martin 10
SWAGAR, Henry 2
SWAGART, George 3, 37
  John 26, 37, 43
  William 19
SWAGER, Henry 37
SWAN, William 57
SWANK, Leonard 52
SWARTS, Frederick 50
  George 50
SWARTZWELL, Mathias 70
SWEET, George 68
SWELLS, William 22
SWIFT, ----- 42
  Joseph 39, 60
SWIGART, Lenard 2
SWITSER, Peter 67
SWITZER, Jacob 10
  John 4, 10, 57, 68, 73
  Peter 10
SWOPE, Lawrence 34, 57
SWOPELAND, Peter 3
SWOPLAND, Peter 37
SWORTZ, Christopher 45

TAGGART, Charles 19, 63
TALKINTON, Jesse 56
TANNER, Stephen 50, 68
TANTLINGER, Henry 12
TARWATER, Jacob 73
TAYLOR, Edward 37
  John 30, 47
  Mathew 43
  Matthew 37
  Samuel 26, 57
  William 43
TEAT, John 63
TEDERICK, John 68
TEDRICK, Frederick 68
TEETS, Yost 68
TEMPLETON, William 31

TEVEBAUGH, Adam 41
  Casper 39
  Jacob 41
THACHAR, Amos 50
THARTS, Joseph 50
THISTLE, Samuel 23
THOMPSON, Adam 30
  David 47, 57
  General 39
  Isaac 30
  James 30, 52
  John 26, 33, 53, 57
  Peter 15
  Samuel 14, 57, 60
  Thomas 52
  William 5, 74
THORLTON, John 30
THORNTON, John 52
THRALL, Joseph 22
TICE, John 26, 43
  William 68
TIPTON, Edward 34, 57
TISON, Mathias 50
TISSUE, William 10
TITTYHEFFER, Christofer 22
TITUS, John 34
  Peter 34, 57
TOBERRY, Thomas 14
TODD, John 3, 37
  Samuel 3
  William 3, 37
TODER, Christian 68
TORBIT, Hugh 30
  John 30
TRAKES, Robert 16
TRAVES, William 52
TRENCH, Daniel 23
TRENT, Captain 39, 54
  William 42, 54
TRIPSHOE, Christoph 41
  Stophel 14
TRUAH, Benjamin 50
TRUAX, Benjamin 22
  Jacob 22, 50
  John 22, 50
  Joseph 50
  Philip 22, 23
  Samuel 22, 50
  Stillwell 19
TRYAR, Christian 68
  John 68
  Michael 68

TRYER, Christian 11
  John 10
  Michael 10
TUCKER, James 41
TUCKMAN Chrisman 5
  Frederick 5
  John 5
TUE, Benjamin 30
TUMBLESON, Benjamin 5
  John 5
TUMBLESTON, Benjamin 73
  Henry 73
  John 73
TUMLESON, John 5
TURBERT, John 47
  Widow 47
TURNER, John 73

UING, John 46
ULERY, Daniel 54
ULY, ----- 34
UNSEL, Abraham 7
  Frederick 7
UTLEY, Jonas 27
  Matthey 26
UTZLER, Christopher 41
  George 14, 41
  Jacob 41
  Martin 14

VALENTINE, Jacob 5, 73
  Lout 67
VANDER, John 32
VANDERIN, John 7, 11, 32, 41, 62, 68
VANDEVADER, Peter 53
VANDIVENDER, Peter 30
VANTREES, John 58
VANTRIES, Frederick 10
VAUGHAN, Thomas 52
VAWN, Thomas 54
VENDOMS, George 5
VETRICH, Coonrod 45
VICKONG, Thomas 32
VICKORY, Thomas 37
VINCENT, Stevens 26

WADSWORTH, Robert 73
WAGEL, Philip 5
WAGGERLINE, Philip 10
WAGGONER, Philip 11
WAIN, John 58
WAKEUP, James 26
WALCOOPE, James 58
WALDREN, Henry 71

INDEX

WALKER, David 26, 43
  George 51, 52
  Jacob 10
  James 8, 45
  John 22, 23, 26, 43
  Widow 51, 68
WALLACE, Ephraim 50
  Patrick 38
  Samuel 30, 31, 32, 33, 42, 47, 54
WALLOCK, Michael 3, 33, 37, 53
WALTER, Barabra 37
  David 73
  Henry 3
  Michael 8, 45
WANE, John 26
WANGER, Jacob 45
  Peter 45
WARD, Edward 5, 74
  John 61
  William 26, 43
WARDER, Jeramiah 27, 59
WARFORD, Henry 22
  James 22, 51
  Widow 22, 50
WARNER, Henry 26, 58
  Paul 26
WARNIEF, Philip 73
WARRAN, Edward 73
WASON, Robert 47
  William 52
  Williams 31
WATSON, James 26
  William 14, 31, 52, 60
WATTS, Connard 50
WAUGH, ----- 33, 54
  William 69
WEGLEY, Philip 68
WEIMER, John 45
WEISCARVER, George 3
WELCH, Francis 50
  Nicholas 26
  William 23
WELKER, Andrew 5
WELLS, James 32
  Richard 62
WELSH, Nicholas 43
WENK, Jacob 22
WENSEL, John 61
WERTS, Henry 33
  Peter 37
WERTZ, George 37
  Henry 37
WESOON, Thomas 44

WEST, Henry 3
WESTON, John 15, 60
  Thomas 26, 52
  William 26
WEYLEY, Jacob 70
WEYMER, Adam 12
  Isaac 12
  John 8
WHARTEN, ----- 29
  ----- 30
WHARTON, ----- 16, 27, 33, 38, 47, 53, 54, 55, 58, 74
WHIPKEY, John 22
WHITE, Francis 15
  Hugh 22
  John 8, 15, 60
  Richard 8
  Susannah 15
  Thomas 74
  William 15
WHITEINGER, Francis 26, 58
WHITLOCK, Thomas 8
WHITNELL, Robert 14
WHITSTONE, Henry 12, 41
  Michael 16, 60, 61
WHORAH, Adam 51
WICKAMS, Samuel 41
WIGFIELD, Benjamin 12, 41
  Joseph 41
WILDS, William 43
WILEY, William 58
WILHELM, William 51
WILKER, Andrew 73
  Paul 5
  Powel 73
WILKEY, Robert 22
WILLCOCKS, James 52
WILLHELM, Alexander 73
  George 73
  Jacob 3, 37
WILLIAM, John 41
  Robert 19
  Shadric 41
  Thomas 22
WILLIAMS, Benjamin 62
  Enoch 19
  Henry 13, 41, 58
  James 3, 37, 52
  John 52, 70
  Robert 69
  Thomas 14, 50
  William 22

WILLSON, George 47, 58
  Isaac 64
  James 45
  John 19, 47, 63
  Robert 64
  Thomas 47, 64
  William 44, 47, 65
WILLT, John 41
WILSON, Charles 19
  David 31, 52
  Elizabeth 15
  George 26, 31
  Hill 19
  Hilley 63
  Jacob 27
  James 8, 14, 26
  John 26, 31, 43
  Joseph 50
  Thomas 14, 60
  William 5, 19, 31
  Zebulon 60
WIMER, Frederick 45
  George 45
  Isaac 70
  Jacob 45
WIMMER, Adam 69
  John 70
WINGER, Christopher 32
  Jacob 10, 68
  Peter 10, 68
WINK, Jacob 51
WINSEL, John 32
WINTER, Stephen 19
WINTON, William 26
WISECARVER, George 37
WITEHAM, Matthew 23
WOLF, Philip 37
  Reinhart 3
  Rinehart 37
WOLFKILL, Conrad 19
WOLLERY, Daniel 34
WOOD, Joseph 38
  Major 39
  Mr. 65
  Sacksarel 62
  Thomas 13, 73
WOODS, George 1
  Thomas 69
  William 51
WOOLBACH, Godfrey 73
WOOLF, George 45
WORKMAN, Joseph 73
  William 5, 73

INDEX

WORLEY, Achor 13
  Anthony 42
  Ezekiel 41
  Ezekil 41
WORREL, Isaac 52
WORRIL, Isaac 31
WORTH, Thomas 31
WRIGHT, David 61
  Henry 7
  Joel 22
  John 41, 58
  Samuel 7, 44
  William 60
WYMER, Frederick 8

YAGER, Peter 22
YEAKY, Henry 22
YEATS, Elizabeth 41
YEODER, Christian 32
  John 32
YODER, John 68
YOTHER, Christopher 61
  John 61
YOUNG, Adam 13, 41
  Casper 61
  James 5, 73
  John 52
  Lodwick 45
  Ludwick 8
  Michael 51, 64
  Thomas 31
  William 5, 26, 73
YOWLER, Isaac 68

ZANTLINGER, Cathrine 70
ZECHMAN, John 10
ZIMMERMAN, Yeost 10
ZUCK, Jacob 10
  Yost 10

www.ingramcontent.com/pod-product-compliance
Lightning Source LLC
Chambersburg PA
CBHW071156090426

42736CB00012B/2355